WE WERE

GROWING UP I

FORTIES AND FIFTIES

Howard Gee

Acknowledgments

To Carmine without whom this book would never have been written.

To our son in law Kelvin for his time and technical knowledge he has kindly given.

To our grandchildren
Jamie, Lucy, Carla and Maisie whom we hope in years to come will enjoy reading the stories of a past childhood.

Biography

Howard Gee was born and educated in Edinburgh and has worked, travelled and lived throughout Europe and the Far East with his family. Howard is married to Carmine and they have two grown up children and four Grandchildren who are now all very happy to be living in the shadows of the Wallace Monument near Stirling and the magnificent Ochil Hills.

Whilst serving in the Scots Guards, Howard was selected into the Army Physical Training Corps and was involved on active service with the Brigade of Gurkhas in Borneo and with other regiments throughout troubled areas of the world. He served in all Non Commissioned Ranks including Regimental Sergeant Major and was commissioned into the APTC in 1980. He is now retired and writing his memoires; the first of which is titled 'We Were Only Bairns'.

WE WERE ONLY BAIRNS

Works by Howard Gee

We Were Only Bairns
Growing Up In Edinburgh In The Forties And Fifties

(Book 1 from the 'There and Back' series)

Boots and Bearskins
Life As A Recruit In The Scots Guards

(Book 2 from the 'There and Back' series)

From Porridge To Paddy Fields
A Scottish Family Living In Hong Kong

(Book 3 from the 'There and Back' series)

Table of Contents

Preface

I was born in 1941 in a front facing top flat tenement building in Edinburgh within the sound of the Castle's famous One O'clock Gun. Stables at the top of the street were the main reason that horses were a regular sight; pulling carts of milk, coal, ceremonial coaches and drays from the nearby brewery but the pomp and majesty of the Household Cavalry en route to Edinburgh Castle, trotting up and down Grove Street annually during the Edinburgh Tattoo was a lasting memory for all the children who lived in or around the street. When Roy Rogers the famous cowboy, brought his even more famous horse Trigger to Edinburgh, the stable entrance was mobbed with excited children and inquisitive adults.
The sawmill, the bakery, the sweetie factory, the brewery and the rubber mill hooters went off early morning and at tea time to start and end the day's work respectively. A noisy stream of people wearing caps, overalls, and clogs or studded boots streamed up and down the street talking endlessly. At night and weekends they were replaced by the young folk wearing the latest fashions making their way up to and back down from the Palais de Danse at Fountainbridge, known locally as the Palais.
The street was a honeycomb of escape routes and when being chased, children could run into tenements, down back stairs, through disused cellars and basements, into back greens, climb walls and disappear only to emerge a few streets further away.
Bookie's runners stood on the corner but had to be alert and move fast when either the lorry emptying the pig's bins (full of tattie peelings and rotting food) arrived or their lookout informed them that the policeman on the beat was heading their way. It was the policeman's duty to arrest them for receiving money from punters for the betting on horses. When lifted they were normally taken to the High

Street Police Station where they spent the night in a cell before appearing in court the following morning, fined and released around dinner time.
Shops in the street were kept busy and women en route to the public wash house at Tolcross rushed up and down with their bundles of washing tied to rickety old prams whilst absorbing or giving out the latest gossip. Controlling their prams with one hand whilst holding a woodbine in the other was truly an art only achieved by continuous practice.
It was a tough upbringing on the streets which were main arteries of life where people struggled to feed, clothe, raise their families and cope with the difficulties of the aftermath of war. It was often determination, friendship, caring for one another and a good sense of humour that took them through each day.
Grove Street was one such community and I have tried to share the memories of a passing way of life for all to enjoy.

Chapter 1 - Nature's Waste

'Hurry up, they're coming, they're coming.' shouted Billy, stretching his vocal cords to their limit whilst straining his neck upwards to the top landing inside the tenement building.
I heard him, opened my door and bounded down the stairs two at a time, bucket and shovel in my hands; almost knocking Billy over. He had his pail and long handled broom at the ready as we ran down the bottom flight of stairs and out into the evening sunshine bathing Grove Street. I had entered the world within the sound of the One O'Clock Gun fired from Edinburgh Castle daily.
A small crowd had lined the pavements either side of the street, cheering and clapping. Most of the front facing tenement houses had their heavy curtains pulled aside to let mothers and the elderly hang out the windows for a better view.
Riding down the cobbled street in their full majestic glory was the Household Cavalry with their helmets and breast plates sparkling in the evening sunshine. With their white breeches tucked into their thigh length black riding boots, the troopers were resplendent bobbing up and down in their saddles to the melodic accompaniment of their jingling spurs. The ebony black horses with their brushed coats and glittering horse regalia looked magnificent as their manes gently waved to and fro like the locks of a mermaid's hair as she surfaces from the deep. Down the hill they trotted from the stables en route to the Castle where the Edinburgh Military Tattoo was performed each night as the major attraction of the Edinburgh Festival.
Myself and Billy MacLeod, as two eight year old boys, , paraded on the front steps of the tenement; standing to attention, chests out, shovel and broom pressed into our

sides as if on parade. We were bursting with pride. The Household Cavalry riding down our street had me mesmerised. I knew then, that when I grew up, I wanted to be a soldier.
I glanced down at Billy who, overcome with excitement, had dribbled down his trouser leg. As he was wearing short trousers, a visible stream of water was running into his socks.
Suddenly as the horses in the rear rank and the police mounted escort rode by, I blinked, nudged Billy back into the real world and we jumped down the stairs taking up the position at the rear of the parade.
We swung our broom and shovel into action filling our buckets with steaming hot smelly dung trying not to slip on it as we lifted it from the cobbles and tipped it into our buckets.
'Oh what a pong,' said Billy holding his nose. 'We should have brought clothes pegs.'
Nothing encouraged rhubarb to grow quicker and stronger than heaps of nature's waste, especially when delivered by the carrier from the elite stables at Windsor. People with gardens and allotments couldn't get enough of the quality dung; the going rate was about three pence a bucket as after all it was fresh.
It had been announced on the wireless that the world renowned cowboy, Roy Rogers and his even more famous horse Trigger were coming to visit Edinburgh and Trigger was to reside at our stables.
'Now that would be quality dung, attracting a higher rate of sale', I thought to myself. The gang would have to review prices at a later date especially as it had been agreed to give the income to Mr. and Mrs. Slovenski who had come from Poland but had lived in the street for many years.
Their daughter, Elaina?, had been born with the terrible disease of polio and had to wear callipers on both legs. The family were saving for a special wheelchair for Elaina, and a ramp to be built leading up to their main door flat. The whole street had rallied round to assist them in raising the required funds. This was a good and worthwhile project for the gang. Everyone in the street wanted to help and our

gang had decided to do just that. Some said that we were little angels.
Others had different thoughts.

Chapter 2 -The Pub

It was about tea time when a top flat window opened and my mother's voice bellowed out, 'Howard, come up for yer tea now!'
'Och ma', I replied, 'not now'.
'Now!!' she bawled, 'This very minute.'
'I'd better go Billy. See you tomorrow morning. Thank goodness it's Saturday; no school. We can go round the doors and sell the goods before it has lost its freshness. That's two extra loads shovelled up tonight. We'll take one each up the stairs now and store them in the morning. That's nine bucketfuls in total this week. Great!'
'Right Howard, see you tomorrow morning,' he replied.
Reaching the top flat out of breath through carrying my heavy load I shouted as I turned the key in the door.
'It's me Ma, I'm here. Is tea ready?'
'What's that smell?' she shouted. 'Yuk! for goodness sake, what's in that bucket? No don't tell me.' she said with her well-practised despairing voice whilst throwing her arms heavenwards as if seeking divine help.
'It's dung ma from London and I thought that I would just keep it in the coalbunker overnight for safekeeping. I knew that you wouldn't mind.'
'The coalbunker is in the kitchen,' she screamed; again throwing her hands into the air, 'and don't use that word dung!!'
'You told me not to say horses sh...!!'
'Don't you dare' she yelled before I could finish the word. 'It's called manure and get it out of here this second. Take it down to the back green and put it with the rest of that pile you've been gathering, no doubt for distribution.'
"But ma.'
'Take it now,' she screamed. 'Right away, this very instant'.
'Are you sure I can't leave it until tomorrow morning?' I

pleaded. The look from my mother said it all and confirmed her negative stance on the matter.
'Can I leave it in the outside lobby, just till the morning?'
'No! no! no! and I'm telling your dad about your argumentative behaviour, your daft ideas and your plain impudence, And scrub your hands before you come back into this house. I'll leave a pail of soapy water and a scrubbing brush outside the front door.'
Without looking back, I shouted, 'Okay Ma, all right.' Losing the battle and wondering what impudence meant as I closed the outside door and made my way down the stairs to the passageway leading to the cellars and the back green.
Seeking a suitable hiding place, I realised that mum did not appreciate the quality of goods that I had in my possession and that if they were pinched overnight valuable income for the week would be affected and my status with my pals would be reduced. I hid the priceless dung in one of the bogey holes (old disused coal cellars) deep in the basement of the tenement. Children were warned by their parents not to go into that particular one in case they caught scarlet fever, have to go to hospital and maybe even go to meet the angels. It was the perfect hiding place for our cache of dung.
Back up the stairs as I entered the house, the key always being kept in the front door. I heard the voice.
'Have you washed yer hands and where's my bucket?'
'I've hidden it in the back green like you told me ma but I'll bring it up tomorrow and wash it so that it will be clean for carrying the coal.'
'Are you being cheeky again?' she said looking me in the eye and daring me to say something clever and witty.
'No ma,' I said sheepishly.
'Better not,' she said squeezing out the words between her teeth.
'Have you washed your hands?' she asked again.
'No ma but I will now.'
'Now!' she screamed 'And before you sit down for tea, go over to the pub and tell yer dad that his tea is ready.'
'He might be playing dominoes.' I said.

'If he wants his tea, he'll have to decide which he prefers; his dominoes or his tea. Tell him that it will be cold unless he comes right away. Hurry up and get back here before yours gets cold.' 'Och!' she mumbled, 'what is it about boys and men?'

'Right ma,' I shouted showing a willingness to please. Of course I had to wait outside Ryrie's Pub door until I could ask someone going in to pass the message to dad or try to catch his eye in the crowded bar as the door swung open. Sometimes I was successful in jamming my foot into the gap before it closed.

Often drastic measures were required to reach dad and I had to crawl on my hands and knees across the sawdust floor, through the bar, ducking below the sight of the ever vigilant bar staff. Luckily the barmen were usually pulling a pint of beer with a small frothy top as Scots customers liked it; value for money they said.

Chameleon-like eyes of the staff could only see what was happening around the bar and not on the floor. Men tended to stand drinking their beer continuously moving and fidgeting about as they downed their refreshing pints of draught beer and their follow up dram of whisky. A hauf and a hauf (half pint of beer and a half of whisky) was a common request; so my dad told me.

As I crawled between shuffling feet, I think bets were often taken as to how far I would get before being spotted and thrown out by the scruff of my neck. Sometimes I would be given sixpence for my efforts from the newly opened Friday night pay packets. Men worked hard and a Friday night stopover at the pub allowed them to laugh at old jokes, hear the up-to-date news, socialize and relax before going home for tea. Those who stayed on to around eight o'clock would often pick up hot rolls from the near-by bakers as a peace offering. My mother said that thirteen rolls were usually give as the bakers dozen.

Like the pony express, somehow I always managed to get the message through to dad.The sights, sounds and stories of the pub were enhanced each time that I had to call dad for his tea. According to dad on a Saturday night, after the football, the pub was always packed, and tills

would be ringing fast and furious.
The Green and The Pink newspapers containing the afternoon football results would be sold and bought outside the front doors of the pub. Inside, the Salvation Army gave out their newspaper 'The War Cry' for a voluntary donation and customers enjoyed a bit of banter with the young ladies who tied their bonnets daintily under their chins. Cheery customers popped their loose change into the collection tins which helped to alleviate suffering from the poor children and people around the world.
When football results had spread around the bar, friendly rivalry between Heart's and Hib's supporters would commence. As we lived on the flight path to Tynecastle my dad was a Heart's supporter and maroon scarves hung on the coat hooks in our lobby.
Happy days!

Chapter 3 - My Family

I began to think about the cold winter evenings when the whole family had sat around the coal fire making toast on the brass toasting fork. Mum and Dad would answer our questions and tell us about how and where they met.

My dad was over 6ft. tall, hardworking, honest and an upright man with strong views and principals about people's rights. His full title was Howard Harry Gee and he was known to all as Big Howard. He was born in the Dummydykes area of Edinburgh and by all accounts, he was a good goalkeeper for St. Bernard's football team and sang in the Old Saint Pauls Episcopal Church Choir. His vocal qualities, I could not verify but as he sang in the choir for a number of years, I presumed that he was up to the standard required by the Choir Master. His shirt sleeves were generally rolled up and his belt complimented his braces in keeping his trousers up. Like most men of his day he wore a bunnet to keep his head warm but unlike my uncle Willie he didn't use his bunnet to waft over his tea which he had poured from his cup into his saucer to cool it down before drinking it.

Mum was average height, plump of stature and wore curlers in hair at night. Sometimes the curls were encouraged into place by using her small iron tongs that had been heated on the fire before being twisted around a lock of hair to produce a curling effect which was aided by the wearing of a hair net in bed overnight. A friend once sold her a rubber roll-on corset and although I wasn't sure exactly what its purpose was, I didn't think that it made much difference. I entered the world on the 10 December 1941 with the assistance of the midwives of the Golden Jubilee Nurses and was christened Howard James Grant Gee in the Old Saint Pauls Church, Currubber's close, off the High street.

My earliest recollection of life was that of my mother placing me into a large look alike Easter Egg which was resting on the coalbunker at the kitchen window. She confirmed to me in later years that this was the standard safety drill for babies whenever the sirens warned of the imminent attack by German bombers. I would then be carried downstairs to the back green into an air-raid shelter where we stayed until the danger had passed.
The rubber mill was situated in Fountainbridge near the McEwen's Brewery at the top end of Grove Street and was a prime target for the bombers. Mothers took their children to the mill shop to buy wellies at cheap rates and I could never understand why the Germans thought that stopping the production of wellies would help their war effort.
Alistair Crook (Ally) was born on 12 February 1943 and Eleanor Willis decided to join the family on 21 February 1950.
Like most families at that time, we didn't have much money but we were clothed, well fed with a roof over our heads and were a happy family ; most of the time.
Dad loved political discussions but sometimes they would turn into heated arguments when friends were visiting us and generally after a few beers and a dram of whisky or two.
One night I was bursting for a piddle and reached for the potty under the bed which was standard procedure as the toilet shared by our neighbours was outside in the stair landing. Ally was sound asleep in the other single bed in the big room situated at the end of the lobby. Standing in my bare feet and my underpants; I didn't have pyjamas, I shivered holding the heavy earthenware potty with one hand whilst trying to keep my aim straight with the other. At last I finished. What a relief. I had filled the potty to the brim. I was about to replace it under the bed where it would be retrieved and emptied by mum in the morning when I heard voices in the lobby at the front door. I put the potty down and wondering what was going on I put my ear to the bedroom door. They were not happy voices and words were being spoken in angry tones.
Mum had prepared a supper for some friends of the family.

It appeared that there had been some political discussion which had turned into a heated argument halfway through the meal. Dad had told us that throughout his service in the navy, during the war, he had seen a great deal of children suffering because, there had been no one to look after them, lack of medical supplies, little clothing, starvation, pain and poverty and how we should always appreciate how lucky we were. He strongly believed in fighting for our freedom, and in equal rights for all and was not frightened to speak his mind and often did. Of course not everyone agreed with his views including some of his friends.

I heard a voice 'well if that's your views Howard you are welcome to them along with your hospitality for which we thank you Dorothy.' The front door was opened and I heard footsteps going down the stairs which were lit by gaslight.

'Please don't go' said my mother in a despairing voice. 'At least come in and finish your supper' but her plea was to no avail and I could hear my mum and dad arguing when the door closed.

I darted back across the room and was about to jump into bed when my foot caught the potty, tipped it up and left me standing in a huge puddle.

'Oh no!' I mumbled to myself

Ally now awake thought the situation was hilarious. 'You'll be in trouble,' he mumbled with a stupid grin on his face.

'Shush, go back to sleep and don't say a word.' I growled at him.

I couldn't go through to the kitchen where the cloth and bucket were kept under the sink and where mum and dad were still sharing heated words. I decided on a brainwave moment to slip the pillowcase off the feathered pillow and began mopping up the spreading puddle. The pillowcase was dripping and I had to keep wringing it out back into the potty, working as quickly as I could. Having completed the task I pushed the potty and soaking pillowcase under the bed, jumped in, crawled under the covers and went to sleep.

Later that night I heard my mum tip toe into the room, take down a spare blanket from the cupboard and although neither she nor the blanket were there in the morning, I

knew that she had slept on the settee all night. Two days later all was forgotten and forgiven.
Everyone was speaking and life was back to normal.

Chapter 4 - The Dark Corner

Dad had served in the Royal Navy since the start of the war in September 1939. He was on leave when Armistice was declared on VE Day (Victory Europe) in May 1945 and celebrations throughout Britain began. The street was packed with revellers. The blackout was over, the lights were on, dad was still wearing his naval uniform and from the top of his shoulders I had a fantastic view of happy people in the street singing and dancing accompanied by accordions, bagpipes, bugles, drums and even mouth-organs; not at all in tune but no-one cared nor even noticed.

Everyone was happy, smiling, hugging, kissing and jumping up and down or just holding each other up. Bottles of anything alcoholic were being drunk and when an intoxicated figure fell over the pig's bin and into the swill, everyone had a good laugh.

I now knew that we had won the war and, the Germans were not going to have a victory parade down Grove Street and that I would soon be able to buy sweeties without worrying about mum not having enough coupons left in our family ration book. Almost everything from food to clothing was rationed on a monthly allocation and coupons within the book were torn out and retained by the shopkeepers who exchanged them for cash from government sources. The war had ended and after initial celebrations of freedom, men arrived home in their dark demob suits, soft felt trilby hats, and black shoes carrying a small suite case, compliments of the War Office. It took time to settle back into civilian life and into their old jobs again that is those who still had jobs to go back to. Many who had been wounded had to start looking for new employment in spite of their newly acquired disabilities. Those were the lucky ones who had returned but many families were left grieving

over loved ones who had given their lives for King, country and freedom and were now lying under the earth in some distant land. Others had to care for those who had been physically wounded, blinded, suffered loss of limbs not to mention mentally scarred but we were free and families slowly began to enter a comfort zone and settle down to enjoying life again.
One Sunday, I disgraced myself and the family when an old acquaintance of dad arrived at the house. They had sang in the choir together and the Reverend Macpherson who was a missionary currently serving in East Africa but was now home on vacation, had been invited for afternoon tea in the Edinburgh fashion.
Mum had worked hard preparing the ham and cucumber sandwiches and numerous other mouth-watering dishes not to mention fairy cakes and scones with jam and cream oozing from all sides.
'When can we start mum?' my brother Ally and I asked over and over again.
'When Mr Macpherson has arrived,' was the quick retort. Mum was all keyed up and I wondered if she would curtsey to our guest when he arrived which he duly did on time. Would she? No; she smiled but didn't curtsey.
Dad shook his hand with a warm welcoming grip as old friends do. 'It's great to see you Andrew. You remember Dorothy,' he said stepping to one side.
'Of course I do. Hello Dorothy, my, you are looking splendid.' He gave her a hug and kissed her on each cheek. 'It's lovely to see you both again and thank you for inviting me to your home.' Mum blushing, led the way, down the lobby and into the big room.
He was a tall gangling man wearing a minister's white collar which peeped out from below his long straggly beard and I noticed that his hair was combed to the left side. He wore a dark suit with a matching waistcoat which held a gold watch chain stretching across the small breast pockets. A multi-coloured bright handkerchief drooped out of his top pocket.
We children were introduced to the Reverend and in a grown up manner he shook hands individually with all three

of us taking the opportunity to study us at close quarters with his left eye shut.
'Right!' said mum, 'I think that we are all ready for tea. If you children would lead the way now, through to the kitchen, wash your hands and sit up on the coalbunker at the window with your feet tucked under the table, we adults will follow. Andrew, would you care to use the little boys room?'
'No I'm fine, thank you Dorothy.'
'Thank goodness,' my mother must have thought to herself.
'I bet he's never used an outside stair toilet before,' I thought to myself, seeing the relief in my mother's eyes.
As if reading my mother's mind, the Reverend commented that in Africa, when he required to go to the toilet, he quite often had to go behind the nearest bushes hoping that there wasn't a wild lion in there, snoozing in the shade from the afternoon sun.
As we entered the kitchen we heard the adults talking and laughing.
'What's the little boy's room?' asked Eleanor.
'Shush they're coming,' I whispered.
'Andrew would you care to have the honour of sitting at the top of the table?' asked dad as he pulled out a chair for him to sit down on. 'Dorothy and I will squeeze in at the sides.'
The kitchen was very small and when the table was pulled out from the wall from where it normally stood, moving it around with the extensions out was a planned operation but mum and dad were adept at doing just that.
'Can I have a cream cake please?' asked Ally, reaching for it. Mum's reaction had been practiced many times and Ally's hand withdrew as his knuckles were gently but effectively wrapped.
'Behave yourself Alistair and remember your manners,' mum said scowling at him.
'I think we should say grace first.' said a low deep voice from the top of the table.
'Of course,' said my mother 'we always do.' she lied as the words rolled off her tongue although to be fair we did say it together on special occasions.

'Now children sit up and bow your heads.' dad said supporting my mother.
From the top of the table came words 'For what we are about to receive, may the Lord make us truly thankful.'
We all joined in with, 'amen!'
'Did you know those words Howard?'
'Yes sir, we say them at school dinners every day.'
'What school do you go to?'
'Normal Practising School.' shouted we children in unison. Although Eleanor hadn't yet started school, we had wanted to impress the Reverend by answering the question quickly. Mum had warned us about speaking properly, clearly and confidently.
'That's the Episcopalian School in Orwell Place. I know Reverend Harris from Saint Luke's just around the corner from the school. I believe that he is looking for some new junior members to join his choir.' Said Reverend Andrew
'It's a small school,' confirmed dad 'but discipline and good manners are encouraged and swearing is taboo at all times.'
'Dorothy and Howard, may I say what lovely children you have; they are a credit to you both.' said Reverend Andrew looking at the three little angelic faces at the far end of the table.
Conversation between the adults was in full flow when having finished a number of sandwiches, I asked politely for a cream scone.
'You can all have one now.' said dad. 'I know that you have been waiting patiently.' The large plate full of scones was delicately passed up to our end of the table where Ally selected one for Eleanor and after looking for the biggest one with jam and cream dripping off the sides for himself, he lifted it onto his plate before passing the large plate with the remainder of the scones to me. I tried to take it but my elbow was squeezed into my side and as Ally tried to catch a falling lump of jam he nudged my shoulder. The plate went up in the air, turned upside down showering the table with scones, splattering sandwiches, sausage rolls, fruit loaf, meringues and even mum's fairy cakes everywhere. The front of my newly washed jersey which stretched down

on to my lap looked like a seagull had passed overhead searching for a toilet but hadn't been able to wait.
'Oh! bloody hell.' I shouted, looking down into the disaster lying on my lap.
There was a deathly hush and I knew that all eyes were on me. I had gone too far.
'Howard! Howard!' screamed my mother. 'How dare you use that forbidden language. Where on earth did you hear such language? It certainly wasn't in this house. Leave the table immediately, go out the front door and stand in the corner.'
The cold lobby with the dark corner was between our house and our neighbours the Ritchies. It was a feature of fear and mental torture and no one ever really knew what horrible creatures lurked in that corner, especially at night.
'Yes mum. I'm sorry.' I said and as I eased between the coal bunker, the table, Ally and Eleanor's knees, I bumped the table and sent the milk jug flying, spilling milk everywhere.
'Outside now,' said dad, 'I'll deal with you later.'
As I sheepishly passed the Reverend on my walk of shame, he looked at me, put his hand on my shoulder and said 'Don't worry Howard, it was an accident. No-one was hurt and I'll have a quiet word with mum and dad.' He winked at me as I passed him at the top of the table.
I opened the front door, stepped outside, closed the door behind me and stood in the lonely dark corner; a tear rolled down my cheek.
Our neighbour's door opened and Isobel Ritchie came out. She was a year or so older than me. 'You're not there again Howard!' she said as she took the key off the nail and went into the toilet on the landing.
Another tear rolled down my cheek.

Chapter 5 - A Wholesome Meal

The school was asked to provide some children to sing in the choir at the Sunday morning service of St. Luke's which stood next door to Dalry baths. I was astonished that my name was already on the list when it went up on the school notice board. Reverend Harris was tall which was beneficial to him as he looked down on his flock from his already high perch in the pulpit. He had a large moustache and appeared to be very sombre but he had been known to smile. His hair was grey although his eyebrows were dark and in complete contrast to his stiff white ministerial collar. On one previous occasion, I had been chosen to be one of the Three Wise Men in the school Nativity Play and I was required to wear a dressing gown emulating a flowing robe but as I had never had one, Mr Harris borrowed one for me and I can remember thinking how warm and cosy it was.

Choir practise was Thursday evenings in the church hall from 6-7 pm. On Sunday morning we had our usual briefing in the vestry prior to commencement of the service. We changed into our white surplices and received our final briefing on the order of service, prayers to be said and hymns to be sung. We juniors were once again reminded of the very high standard of behaviour that the congregation expected from us throughout the service. Having ensured that our faces were wiped and our hair combed as instructed, we lined up behind Cuthbert, an older boy who had a posh accent and carried the tall crucifix. There were eight boys mostly from my class at school not including snooty Cuthbert. We were followed by the ladies and gents of all ages, shapes, sizes and looks: about twenty in all. The minister brought up the rear of the procession and could quickly spot and deal with any semblance of trouble brewing from the front.

As we entered the church from the rear door, the organist

struck up 'Onward Christian Soldiers' with great gusto. Our instructions were to sing the words as written in the hymn books; not our own versions and we were to try and sing in tune. We were not to look at the congregation nor lose the step; not to trip nor trip anyone else and certainly not to be smiling nor sniggering.
We followed pompous Cuthbert down the long aisle and veered left and right into the choir pews exactly as rehearsed, remaining standing until the minister climbed the steps and entered the pulpit where the large bible had been opened and marked in readiness for him. He adjusted some notes, looked up and peered around the pews noting the absentees. He stared ahead for a few moments before speaking. 'Good morning.' He paused for the congregational response.
'Good morning Reverend'
'A warm welcome to you all, especially to those who are with us for the first time today.' he continued.
The service progressed in the time honoured sequence but just as the minister had the attention of his flock and was about to commence his sermon, Albert let off a rip roaring loud and smelly fart which sounded like a speedway rider revving up at the start of a race. The smell that engulfed the pews spread quickly up the aisle and into the main body of the Kirk. It was a mixture of rotten eggs, leaking sewage and a sickly vomit. It was difficult to tell which side of the pews the sound had erupted from but all eyes immediately looked to where we boys were sitting. We looked at each other trying to source the blame before bursting into uncontrollable laughter. The congregation fell silent and were whispering to each other whilst shaking their heads in disgust. The minister scowled at us, kept his dignity and continued with his holy lesson keeping one eye on the congregation whilst his other roamed our pews. He was obviously trained in such matters.
All solemnity of the service went out the window, unfortunately the smell didn't and it circulated around the main body of the congregation who sat in silence trying not to breathe in.
After the service nobody owned up in spite of the minister's

inquisition although suspicion unfairly fell on me as the ringleader and as having orchestrated the whole disgraceful act.
All eight boys, not Cuthbert of course, were disrobed and drummed out of the choir and that was that. Afterwards Albert told us that for dinner the previous day, the family had broth made from a whole sheep's heid and for tea, tripe from a cow's stomach with potatoes and onions; usually considered to be a wholesome meal.

Chapter 6 - Behind Bars

One Saturday morning, I had a fight with a boy about my own age. He was from another school and lived up the hill near the sweetie factory. As we were playing football in the front street he just picked up our ball and ran off with it. As it happened the ball belonged to Titch Cameron but I was the fastest runner and took off after him. He went off crying and we got our ball back but little did I realise that I had set the wheels in motion for big trouble.

On the Monday afternoon coming home from school, I was trying not to scuff my shoes, and prevent my schoolbag from falling off my shoulder as I kicked an imaginary ball into the net; just like my Hearts heroes Willie Bauld and Jimmy Wardhaugh, known to all supporters as Twinkletoes. Like my pals, I had an ex. army khaki coloured school bag that had held a gas mask which was carried everywhere by people during the war in readiness to combat a gas attack and which were now sold very cheaply in the Army and Navy Stores.

I had just about reached the stair when who comes charging down the hill shouting and pointing at me with threatening gestures, was that fore-mentioned boy. Immediately behind him was his big brother who looked about twelve feet tall and eight feet wide. Remembering David and Goliath, I found a hidden energy; thought again and bolted up my stair hoping that they would know the unwritten law of not following one's quarry into home territory in case there was an even bigger enemy waiting in ambush.

I reached the top landing with the large windows looking down on to the main street. Iron bars were in place to prevent inquisitive children from getting too close to the beckoning panes of glass but I knew how to push my head through the bars, turn it to the left and right again and my nose would be pressing on to the glass. I stopped for breath before looking down through the window at the raging gorilla and his chimp in the street looking up at me and jumping up and down. I knocked on the window and made a very rude gesture, confident now that they were not going to come up the stair after me. They shook their fists, made even ruder gestures at me and went back up the street mumbling to each other.

I laughed out loud for the benefit of my pal Jimmy who had heard the commotion and come out from his house on the first landing to see what was happening. I turned my head to relate the story to him and stopped laughing when I realised that I couldn't pull my head back through the bars. Panic set in.

Jimmy's older brother Billy came out to help and as I twisted my neck and shoulders, he pulled at my legs. Encouraged vocally by Jimmy, I strained, held my breath and strained again; remembering the time when I had taken part in the tug of war at the Sunday School Picnic. Ugh! It was to no avail. Billy went to fetch my mother who went for Mr Dougherty who lived across the landing. He almost succeeded in setting me free but I had to scream when I felt my head leaving the top of my neck. Mrs Dougherty went downstairs and across the street to seek help from Mr Michael the only person in the street who had a telephone. He arrived and said that he had been a chef in the army and thought that he could solve the problem by spreading cooking fat on my ears and trying to twist my head almost 360 degrees but it appeared that no one would authorise the action. As Billy pulled on my legs again, my right shoe came off. Jimmy was bawling and shouting for help whilst my mother who had heard the commotion appeared from the house. I was told afterwards that she had tried to help by placing her hands over her eyes, shaking her head and sobbing.

The Cleaneasy man who wore a turban turned up with his case full of brushes sponges and an array of bottles with coloured oils and liquids called for everyone to stand back and let the dog see the rabbit. A soapy liquid was squeezed around my head and neck running down the

inside of my vest like a sliding volcanic river on the move, causing a cold clammy feeling.
With his army training, Mr Michael now weighed up the problem again and decided to stamp his authority on the situation. He edged through the neighbours who had appeared on the landing scurried downstairs and squeezed through the gathering crowd on the pavement who were looking up and pointing to me at the window. One woman looked upwards as she said a prayer whilst another blessed herself. Mr Michael had decided to use his telephone and called the fire brigade who came screaming down Morrison Street in their big red fire engine, ladders hanging off the back and bells ringing out to the world. They turned left into Grove Street and screeched to a halt outside the stair. The police arrived in their Black Maria and rolled in behind them. A large crowd had gathered in the street and on hearing the bells the minister from the nearby St. David's Church had joined the throng to offer his assistance and blessed help.
The firemen unrolled their hoses whilst others with their helmets on and axes at the ready ran up the stairs to review the situation. The bars were prised open and my head popped out. A huge cheer erupted and applause continued for several minutes as I waved and smiled to all below.
My mother, who had a very red face and steam coming out of her ears, thanked the firemen and all concerned for their assistance before she grabbed me by the scruff of my collar and marched me up the steps into our house on the top landing. She bawled and shouted at me, pushed me into the wee bedroom and clipped me round the ear before slamming the door shut. She didn't seem at all pleased to have me back safe and well.
Oh dear! Big trouble this time. I just knew it. That night my dad put me over his knee and walloped me with a slipper. It wasn't only my neck that was red that night.
Well deserved, I suppose.

Chapter 7 - Gang Huts And Halloween

In the 1940's, Edinburgh had few cars on the roads and children playing in the streets were more likely to get knocked down by a horse pulling a milk cart or a dray full of heavy beer barrels. Grove Street was a warren of basements, cellars and stairs with long dark passageways leading into bogey holes where supposedly bogeymen lived.

Families shared back greens housing bomb shelters which were relics from the war and these with the front streets were our playgrounds. Low and high walls surrounded the greens where washing dried on blowy days and we children dug holes, made gang huts, climbed up, walked along and dreeped down the walls. Iron railings and fences were everywhere but twisted, missing and broken rails provided escape routes for cowboys being chased by Indians or pirates and musketeers attacking or retreating from skirmishes, not to mention quick escapes for the boys being chased by girls who wanted to play at shops or doctors and nurses.

Women would hang out their windows, shouting and shaking their fists as fleeing children ran through lines of newly washed sheets and clothes drying in the breeze. Washing lines were tied to and ran between standing upright metal poles. The lines were supported in the middle by long wooden poles which dug into the ground whilst the other end in the shape of a V, pushed the rope upwards ensuring that long sheets were kept off the ground and clothes were aired. Often a basin of water would be tipped on us as we ran below windows heading for escape routes through doors leading into newly washed passageways

and out into the freedom of the front streets leaving verbal abuses trailing behind; 'I'll tell your mother Howard Gee,' women hanging out of windows would shout and they did.
Cellars with old bits of carpets on the floor, boxes for tables and chairs made perfect gang huts. Blankets hung over doorways ensuring that the outside world was unaware of strategic decisions being made within. Flickering candles provided the creepy atmosphere for ghost stories and secret meetings. Only special prearranged knocks and passwords allowed entry to the inner sanctum although 'keep out' signs were often ignored by nosey adults.
As the hut had to be kept tidy, swept out regularly, burnt out candles replaced, in conjunction with numerous other chores, girls were allowed into the gang but their acceptance had to be voted on by the committee and I had the final say. Once they had proved their trust they were allowed to go errands for pies, chips, lemonade and sweeties depending on the availability of funding. Doll's prams and nurses uniforms were barred; equality for both sexes hadn't yet reached the gang huts. All members of the gang had to take and be bound by the sacred oath of loyalty or be banished to a distant land forever.
Loyalty was extremely important especially during the bonfire season when rival gangs from other streets would attack and try to steal our hard earned collection of flammable rubbish for bonfire night on the 5th November each year. The stair with all its nooks and crannies became the focal point.
One night, I was coming home from the cubs; heading for the top flat, whistling as always up the dark stair. As was often the case, the stair gas lamp had not been lit and as I turned the first corner there was a swishing, striking noise and a huge light lit up a white ghostly face. 'Aaaaaah!!,' it shrieked.
I screamed and ran past the ghostly apparition imagining bony fingers clutching at the back of my neck. I didn't stop until I reached my door on the top landing.
'You're alright laddie,' shouted a voice behind me with a sneering laugh. On his way downstairs to the pub Willie Dingwell had decided to stand in the dark corner, strike a

match and light up his pipe but holding the match too long, he had burnt his fingers and let out that haunting shriek. What a fright. Hazards of living up a stair, I suppose; but I was relieved. I thought that it might have been a lost soul coming into the stair in readiness to celebrate Halloween.

'You look as if you have just seen a ghost,' my mother said.

I shook my head as I removed my cub cap and neckerchief whilst placing my woggle in a safe place.

As the end of October approached and the bewitching hours of Halloween were creeping in, plans for guising were laid out by the gang. The draw was made as to who would join each team of threes or fours (boys and girls mixed).

Turnips had to be gouged out with wide eyes, triangular nose and jagged teeth to allow the light from the candle to shine through, portraying a gruesome monster of the night. The top of the turnip which had been cut off was held in place by string passing through a hole at the side where the ears would normally have been. It was then passed up through the cap and down the other side, ensuring that the string was long enough in the middle to carry the turnip around. A firm top would help to keep the candle lit by protecting it from the wind.

Everyone joining in would choose their fancy dress which ranged from pirates, cowboys and nurses to ghosts, monsters, vampires and other scary creatures from the dark world. The latter group was always more popular. Decisions had to be made as to which jokes were going to be told, songs to be sung, streets and stairs to be covered by which groups and who was to be the leader of each group, carrying the bucket for the sweets and money to be dropped into. The spoils were always shared out at the end of the night.

As bells were rung, doors knocked on and opened, we would respond by bursting into a well-rehearsed song. Dressed in a dark wig and face blackened with soot taken from the lum, white lips, white gloves and a bow tie, Hughie (Shuggie) Clelland was a double for Al Jolson. When he got down on one knee with outstretched arms and sang

'Mammy' women broke into tears of joy and the money just poured into the bucket. It was the luck of the draw but Shuggie always seemed to squeeze into my team.
At Halloween parties, dooking for apples was popular. You were blindfolded as you knelt on and leaned over the back of a chair with a fork dangling from your mouth, aimed roughly at the swirling apples in the basin or tin bath below. With a bit of luck, the fork would pierce an apple which was yours to keep but even more popular was kneeling on the floor in front of the bath, ducking one's face into the water and trying to bite into an apple; preferably one that didn't already have someone else's teeth marks in it. Biting into a treacle scone dangling on a string held by an adult standing on a chair was also fun but very messy. With arms behind your back and looking upwards at dripping treacle, sheer bravado was required to get your teeth into the scone but what a great source of laughter for all.
Fun, games, enjoyment and laughter were memories of Halloween.
'Oh! Sweets and money too; I nearly forgot them.'

Chapter 8 - The Punishment

Every year the 5th November meant thoughts turning to fireworks, Guy Faulks, bonfires and knocking on people's doors collecting anything that would burn.
Each street formed a gang to protect their own bonfires from raiding parties or to make sorties into other territories and steal from other standing bonfires. Boys carried cudgels or broom handles that were long, not too heavy but appeared threatening to the enemy and would- be marauders.
As the kitchen, rear bedroom windows and stair passageways of the tenements of St. David's Terrace and ours in Grove Street looked on to our back green, each year an alliance was formed with them to collect and protect our bonfire. A large dirt square in the centre of the Terraces where mums usually hung out their washing to dry, was the ideal site and with the blessing of the women, that's where the huge piles of wood, boxes, old beds, mattresses, settees, armchairs and anything that would burn were built up with great skill and tender loving care. Collecting around the area was good fun and one never knew what would happen next.
It was on one of those occasions when four of us on a collecting mission reached the top flat of a stair, rang the bell and waited patiently to utter the immortal words 'anything for the bonfire missus?' A tall fat woman opened the door wearing a smile on her face and a small black soft hat attached to her head by a protruding hat pin. No jersey, no blouse on. She wore a very large white bra resembling water wings, large blue bloomers that reached down to her knees and a pink corset laced down the front. A red frilly suspender belt held up her long thick brown stockings which disappeared into bright red slippers supporting a pom pom on the toe of each. We looked at each other and

tried not to burst out laughing.
'What is it?' she said.
'Have you anything for the bonfire please?' I asked trying to be polite.
'Oh wait.' she said obviously frustrated as she closed the door.
'I think that we have called at an awkward moment.' I said.
We all burst out laughing and a few rude suggestive comments were made.
The door opened. 'Here's some dolly mixtures.' she said.
Reading our minds, she smiled and closed the door again.
'Ach well.' Jimmy Brown muttered, 'It's all in a day's work.
We might as well share the sweeties out.'
'Aye.' all agreed and burst out laughing again as we made our way to the next stair.
Bangers, rockets with starbursts, cartwheels and roman candles were set off everywhere without due respect to the laws of Health and Safety. Bangers were lit and pushed through letter boxes regardless of who lived within or the state of their nerves.
We pulled the bell outside the front tenement entrances whilst simultaneously entering the stairs by using a latch key and when the house owner opened their door we lit and threw a number of bangers into the stairwell creating a noise similar to the opening salvo from the guns at El Alamein. Cartwheels fixed by a pin to outside stair doors spun round in a marvellous splash of colours and fizzy noises but often burnt the paint of the doors albeit in an artistic circular fashion. Rockets were placed in milk bottles or tin cans and pointed at the windows of grumpy people. Bangers were thrown at girls skipping, playing peevery beds or just sitting quietly swapping scraps. Anyone standing around chatting was a target. No real thoughts were given to the plight of neither the elderly nor their pets although we were continually being warned by our parents to be vigilant and very careful with our fireworks.
Patrolling policemen had access to the famous blue police boxes that were strategically situated around the streets. Intelligence was regular and collated quickly. The whereabouts of rogues were known and crimes were often

prevented before they even happened. Required assistance was prompt and policemen on the beat gained an inner strength on cold winter nights by being able to enjoy a hot cup of tea whilst writing up their notes. Helmets were replaced by flat caps with black and white dicing and the local bobby was respected by most adults and their children.

We youngsters didn't appreciate the dangers to ourselves or others that fireworks could cause; scars were often burned into flesh for life. Daring deeds and fun were foremost in our minds and as the days and nights led up to the 5th November, the bonfires grew bigger and physical battles with gangs from other streets became more frequent. Sometimes twenty to thirty boys and some daring girls would charge into enemy territory, steal some bits from their bonfire and retreat quickly. Revenge was usually swift and conflict ended with a stitch or two on someone's head, or the odd broken finger but it was accepted and there was some pride taken in showing off one's war wounds.

'A bit like shinty matches.' said Callum whose family had moved down from Kingnussie, the shinty capital of the Highlands. We didn't know what he was talking about.

On the night of the 5th a guy would be made and placed on top of the bonfire. A large crowd would gather before the lighting and everyone would comment on the magnificent structure about to go up in smoke. As the flames started at the bottom and gradually leaped up enveloping the guy lots of chatter, laughing and shouting started and continued well into the night. As the fire died down, we roasted tatties in the embers, poking them around with sticks until they appeared to be ready. Usually they were black and burnt on the outside, uncooked on the inside but always tasted fantastic.

The following day would herald in, the reign of peace for another year. Happy days and great fun.

My old school blazer was getting rather worn and my mother finally decided to buy me a new one using her dividend from the CO-OP; her store number was 30641. Next day, I was wearing my new blazer proudly to school when George (Mac) Macdonald decided to put a banger into my pocket where it blew a large hole in it. I immediately thought of heading south, crossing the border and going into hiding for a couple of years to let the dust settle but I knew that my parents would come after me. I was so popular at school that day. Everyone wanted to see my blazer or rather the hole in it; the whole school was talking about.

When I got home that afternoon, I quickly hung my blazer up on the peg in the lobby and decided that I would discuss it with my parents at a convenient time. 10 seconds later, I heard the voice.

'Who did that?'

'Did what mum?'

'Did that.' she shouted pointing at the blazer and more specifically at the hole.

'I don't know mum. I think it was like that when I went to school this morning.' Whack!!; my ear was ringing.

'I can't believe what I'm seeing.' said mum putting her hand inside the pocket and pushing her fingers through the hole to the outside. 'Your dad can deal with this.'

Later that evening, I heard dad's footsteps coming up the stairs and the front door opening. Before he had his cap off with his right hand, his left hand was holding my school blazer. The opportunity to discuss the matter didn't arise and as I bent over the piano stool, I sensed dad loosening off his trouser belt. I took my punishment like a man but my behind was red and sore for a couple of days. I cried silently and knew that I would remember this moment in years to come.

I had to go to school next day with a black patch over my pocket. I spoke to Mac and told him that because he was my best pal, all was forgiven. We had a good laugh but Mac walked around the rest of the month with a black eye.

I had eased through my eighth year of life and slipped comfortably into my ninth.

Chapter 9 - Bath Time

Bath nights were regular twice a week. The large tin bath which doubled up for carting clothes to the wash-house was lifted down from the nail on which it hung in the glory hole (large walk-in storeroom) situated in the lobby. Everything from stepladders and tools, to brushes, mops and shovels were kept in the glory hole; not to mention Dopey the cat and Nellie the budgie; living side by side wasn't a problem for them. A small window leading out to the lobby gave them light and freedom of movement around the house.

On bath nights the well-stocked fire roared up the lum to allow the water in the large blackened kettle and the very large cooking pot to boil on the fire quickly and continuously. There was no other source of heat for neither cooking, frying, boiling nor for providing hot water for washing clothes; not even for washing hands, faces and dirty little grubby knees. Our source of warmth and light for our home came from the fire, complimented by the gas light which swung out from the wall on a long spindle. The brass knob was turned to the 'on' position and the fragile mantle was lit by holding a match up to it. After a loud popping sound the light came flooding in, sweeping over the ceiling and around the walls of the kitchen like Florence Nightingale's lamp lighting up the dark corners of a Crimean hospital ward. Gas mantles had to be regularly replaced from the local dry-salters along with accumulators which allowed wirelesses to operate.

When not in use the kettle and numerous cooking pots were kept at the side of the fire on top of the ebony black grate which mum cleaned and burnished with zeebo and elbow grease (manual hard rubbing) weekly. The flat griddle for frying bacon, eggs, sausages, black pudding, tomatoes and even tattie scones hung in the middle of the

fire on the swee protruding from the chimney breast.
The bath was laid out in front of the roaring fire and my young sister Eleanor was first into the clean water, had a sponge wash and was wrapped in a large towel before being stood in front of the fire to dry off. Ally was next. He had a top up of hot water and a thorough going over with the scrubbing brush from mum. To get into the bath, I had to bend my knees and endure silly remarks about my shyness in trying to cover my little willie with my hands or the sponge, if I could find it. I always hoped that Ally hadn't piddled in the bath. He knew that if he had, he was in big trouble but sometimes as he stepped out he gave me that little brother, silly grin through gritted teeth and silently dared me to accuse him in front of mum. Proving his guilt was very difficult even though I did sometimes see bubbles in the water rising to the surface.
I was scrubbed from head to toe and squeezed into a corner of the fire place with the biggest towel around me. We all had our heads checked for nits and our hair washed in the sink at the cold water tap; the only tap we had although if we were lucky, any warm water left in the kettle was used to rinse our hair. On non-bath nights we stood in the sink, reaching it by standing on a chair. Our knees, legs and feet had the daily grime removed with a large bar of orange coloured coal tar soap in unison with the scrubber.
I well remember my first pair of jeans when I walked around with my hands in the back pockets and felt grown up but the real importance of the occasion was just how much they kept my knees clean and saved a scrubbing at night. They were fantastic and I tried to walk just like John Wayne the famous film star cowboy.
After passing my first swimming certificate I was allowed to take Ally along to Dalry Baths near our school where we could have a hot shower before going in for a swim. A real luxury was being allowed to go upstairs to the slipper baths where a huge enamel bath was filled with boiling hot water by an attendant. When ready, you closed and snibbed the door, having run in enough cold water until you could step into it and sink beneath the surface in sheer bliss. I had to keep shouting to Ally next door to check that he hadn't

drowned. A rap on the door, after about 40 minutes let us know that our time was up and we had to get out; the bath was then cleaned for the next customer.
One day my mother who worked as a charwoman for Mrs Watson whom we called Auntie Watson, told us that we were in for a treat. Whilst Mr and Mrs Watson were away from home for a few days, we were to be allowed to have a proper bath with biscuits and orange juice afterwards. The memory of hot, sweet smelling, soapy bubbles up my nose, the stepping out of the bath on to a soft thick mat, sliding into towelling slippers that had been left as gifts for us and the huge bath towels that wrapped around us two or three times, still lingers with me to-day. Mr J.B. Murray Watson was the editor of the Scotsman Newspaper in Edinburgh and had been invited with Auntie Watson on to the Inaugural Flight of the Brabazon Airliner. It was the best bath we ever had.
At home if I was naughty and I often was, unintentional of course, I would be told off. If however, I was cheeky, rude, downright stubborn or just plain insolent, I could expect a thick ear or a clout from the instrument nearest to my mother's right hand although at times, she could be ambidextrous. These punitive weapons could range from a rolling pin and spirtle (porridge stick) to a soup ladle or dad's belt used for honing his open razor and innumerable other functions. Depending on which direction I jumped so the target area would vary but on most occasions it was the soft fleshy part of my behind that was the successful strike area. This physical skelp was always preferable to standing in the dark corner of the lobby outside our front door or being kept in the house when my pals were out playing; worst of all was losing what little pocket money I had earned that week.
We were taught right from wrong although everything was neither always black nor white. We were disciplined and punished usually in the right way and usually at the right time. We were taught to say 'sorry' when we were in the wrong. Mum always said that we would feel better if we said 'sorry.' Sometimes I did but I got fed up saying it.
'Principals, morals, integrity and freedom of speech for

adults were very important,' said my dad.
We were encouraged to say our prayers and ordered to Sunday school. We were brought up to be honest, wash behind our ears and always to help others in need, especially the old and infirm. Sometimes the elderly would get on our nerves with their mumblings of,
'It wisnae like this in my day. Children were seen and not heard. We had nothing but we were always happy.'
It was probably all true but we did get a bit fed up hearing it. No one in the stair had a car, telephone nor television but the wireless, newspapers and especially word of mouth kept the news circulating reasonably quickly.
Children were by no means angels but were taught to respect their parents and elders. Good manners such as saying 'excuse me, please and thank-you,' were important and giving up one's seat to ladies or old folks on the buses or tramcars was expected and appreciated as well as running to the shops for messages without complaining. Swearing was taboo especially in front of we children, the female form and most of all if your parents were likely to hear you.
Cold winter nights had a special magic when the curtains were drawn and everyone sat around the warm coal fire eating hot buttered toast and listening to the latest adventures in the street. Everyone wanted to know what had gone on at school or work that day. Isobel and Mary who lived next door with their mother Jeanie and old Elly (Mrs Ediminston) who lived across the landing on her own were usually in our house to share these moments in front of the fire.
We would play guessing games, questions and answers, hide the thimble or I spy with my little eye. Dad would tell us stories or read from a book. Mum would sit at the table often talking quietly to Jeanie whose husband had walked out of the house one day and never returned. Isobel was about a year older than me whilst Mary was ages with Ally. Mum and dad had helped Jeanie to cope with life's difficulties of working and trying to bring up two girls on her own. We had two extra sisters and a spare granny in our family.

We listened on the radio to Children's Hour, Riders of the Range, Journey into Space and Dick Barton Special Agent with his two trusty friends Snowy and Jock. Jimmy Shand and his dance band was the Saturday night musical favourite. We made toast on the long brass toasting fork and curled our toes in towards the fire. Mum continually reminded us about the danger of chilblains.

'Who wants chips?' someone would ask; 'or hot rolls?' which were fresh from the baker's oven every Friday night.

'No rolls tonight,' said dad 'it's only Thursday.'

'Oh we're starving,' came the cry from us poor wee hungry souls.

'Alright, alright,' relented dad. 'Who's going for chips?' Usually the two oldest would go. Whilst Isobel and I put our shoes and coats on, the younger ones got washed, pyjamas on and ready for bed.

The chippie was at the top of the street, past the sawmill, over the railway bridge where long rows of vans stood outside Martin's Bakery, waiting to be stocked with fresh loaves of bread, rolls, cakes, biscuits and scones which were baked overnight and delivered to the shops on the early morning runs in time for the breakfast tables. In the wee hours of the morning, the bakers could be seen wearing their white overalls covered in flour, balancing newly filled long wooden trays on their bunnets which sat jauntily on their heads. Fresh inviting smells wafted up the nostrils of the early shift workers en route to the sweetie factory and the rubber mill. To reach Mary and Giovanni's shop, we crossed the street and followed the most appetising smell in the world into their fish and chip shop.

'Buona sera bambini,' Mary would call out as we entered the shop. Some hot chips were laid on top of the counter for us to nibble on whilst our order was taken and made ready. Giovanni always did the frying and the wiping down of the huge fryers from which hot sizzling, brown fat appeared every time he lifted the lids to stir the swirling contents with his long handled frying net before dumping the chips, fish, pies, haggis or white puddings into the hot plate ready for serving.

'What is youra Mamma having tonight?' asked Mary.

'Just chips tonight please, Mary,'
'Salt, sauce and vinegar?' she would ask just before wrapping up the order in a white greaseproof sheet, followed by two pages of newspaper taken from the pile lying on the counter.
'Everything please Mary,' was the standard reply.
'Tella youra mamma and a papa, I aska for them,' said Giovanni looking over his left shoulder but keeping his eye on the bubbling fat in the fryer. 'Arrivederci'
'We will. Thank you. Cheerio Mary; see you later,' we would shout as we left the shop.
When we got home, the chips would be placed in the oven by the side of the fire to keep them warm until everyone was sitting comfortably ready to balance a plate full of piping hot chips on their laps.
'Forks were not needed in my day,' said Elly. 'Fingers were made before forks,' she would remind us as she sat comfortably by the fire where Mary often sat beside her brushing her long hair. She loved the company and the family atmosphere as her eighty plus years stretched out. I remember one Saturday morning my mother giving me the key to her front door and asking me to take a newspaper over the landing to her where she was lying in bed not feeling too well.
'Remember and shout when you go in the front door,' said my mother.
'Good morning Elly. It's Howard. I've brought your paper,' I shouted as I knocked on the bedroom door. With a shawl around her shoulders, she was sitting up in bed but I couldn't take my eyes off the glass on the bedside table full of water with goldfish bobbing up and down. My mother explained afterwards that it was Elly's false teeth in the jar as old folks didn't sleep with them in their mouths in case they swallowed them.
'Oh!' I said.

Chapter 10 - The Stair Toilets

As the evenings closed and the coals turned to ashes, we headed for our beds through in the big room. Coats were placed on top of the blankets to keep us warm and the pig (stone hot water bottle) was placed between the cold sheets to encourage us to get into bed. If visitors arrived unexpectedly, the coats were whipped off the beds and hung back up on their pegs in the lobby.

A string line along the length of the mantelpiece above the fire held a row of socks, hankies, underwear, and other small items of clothing left drying throughout the night in the warmth of the dying embers of the fire. Most of the clothes washed that day had been aired and dried in the back green or on the pulley in the kitchen which was raised and lowered by a controlling rope wound around a hook behind the heavy dark blue curtain; the type which had ensured that the blackout rules were adhered to during the war years.

One day I came home from school to find my mother knee deep in washing; the pulley had collapsed. I laid my schoolbag on a chair, took off my blazer, quickly turned about, grabbed a comic to read, unhooked the key and went outside to the toilet; locking the door behind me. We were lucky that dad was quite a handy man and the pulley was soon in its rightful place beneath the ceiling holding a variety of dangling drying clothes.

Dad was able to save money by replacing worn rubber soles and heels by using his cobblers last to hold the shoe in place whilst he tapped small thin sharp nails into the relevant parts of the shoe. Leather soles required the specialist touch and shoes were handed in to Charlie, the boot maker whose shop lay between the basement where old Mr and Mrs Sheppey lived and the painter and decorators shop in the street. On entering Charlie's shop,

the smell of leather shot up your nostrils and the sound of a rotating belt on a buffing machine created a distinct sound and atmosphere from any other shop in the street. The repair request was written on a label, tied to a shoe lace and the item was placed by Charlie in a row on the repair shelf in a sequence that only he understood.
Perched on his high stool at the counter Charlie looked taller than he was. There was no mistaking his efficiency and cheerfulness towards his customers and as children left his shop he would reach below the counter, produce a sweetie and looking through his small round glasses would say, 'tell your mother that they will be ready for the weekend.' Wearing his long black leather apron with a little hammer in his hand, he always reminded me of one of Santa's little helpers. His left trouser leg which folded up above the knee, told the world that he was disabled in spite of his incredible mobility. He was adept at balancing on his wooden crutch padded under his left arm whilst carrying out his craft up and down the shop. No one was sure how Charlie had received his wound resulting in the loss of his leg during the war and he never spoke of it.
At home in the morning, the ashes from the fire would be shovelled up, placed into a metal ash bucket kept in the glory hole until placed outside with the normal rubbish on collection days. Tattie and vegetable peelings were taken across the street to the pigs bins which stood beside the lamppost outside the Antediluvian Order of Buffaloes Club known as the 'BUFFS'. The swill was collected once a week by a pig farmer from the outskirts of Edinburgh.
On cold mornings, going to the toilet on the landing outside the front door was indeed an effort and unless very desperate, one tried to wait until fully clothed or even someone else had warmed up the seat. First out to the toilet in the morning took the potty from under the bed to empty it. Usually filled to the brim, a delicate steady control of the hand was required to reach the front door, especially when reaching for the toilet key on the nail behind the door. The sensible action was to place the potty down on the floor prior to opening the door, step outside, lift up the potty, and close the door without spilling a drop. Numerous

sequences were tried and disasters were common. Turning the key in the toilet door and entering the hallowed room without spilling a drop was truly a feat indeed and rarely ever happened.

The huge front entrance door of the stair lay open permanently and leaned into the inner wall like a drunken man on a Saturday night catching his breath and arranging his legs before tackling the stairs upwards to the houses on the various landings. The stairs leading downwards to the bowels of the tenement; past the disused bogey holes and cellars, led to a long dark passageway, pointing the way to the steps leading up to the back green where washing dried when the sun was out and children played as an alternative to the front street.

On the first landing two families were housed in each of the alcoves to the left and right; four families in all. Two outside toilets had small windows for ventilation opening on to the landing. As one passed en-route to the top landing, it was quite usual to be able to tell who the occupier of either or both of the toilets were. The giveaway clues were cigarette or pipe smoke coming out of the windows, grunts and groans, mumblings, a rustling of newspaper or reading material, lights on, lights off, someone knocking on the door and shouting "Hurry up, the children are waiting to go to bed or even school."

The smells were worse at weekends, probably because men consumed more quantities of alcohol at the pubs and on the way home were bursting for the toilet. Not having time to lift the seat or not even bothering, uncontrolled urination and spraying over the walls did cause an unhygienic smell which tended to pass unnoticed by the guilty party due to the long sigh of relief within. Upon the discovery of soaking wet trousers and uncontrollable buttons, foul language poured out of the toilet windows and into the hearing systems of anyone passing up or down the stairs.

Then there was the proverbial scream from a desperate child, 'there's nae paper left.' Daily newspapers were cut into squares and neatly hung up on a hook within reach of children. The news was often read and pictures looked at

before being flushed away forever.
The top landing toilets didn't have lights as it must have been presumed that the gaslight from the stair would flood in through the ventilation holes at the top of the toilet doors, allowing papers, comics and private documents to be read even in the dimmest of lighting. In the evenings, torches allowed the reading to continue. Keys were kept inside the houses to prevent the use of toilets by coalmen, milkmen, paperboys, postmen, telegram boys, gasmen, salesmen, roofers, ragmen, plumbers, joiners, electricians, ministers, priest's doctors, nurses and stray children, all who used our stair. 'Oh!' Not to forget chimney sweeps, Jehovah Witnesses and Mormons. The problem was when a key got lost and someone especially a child was bursting. The situation became serious and often police sniffer dogs were about to be called in when the key would be found or a spare turned up.
What a relief for many a child.
Toilets had to be kept clean along with the stairs and a card was hung on house front door handles to remind all concerned that it was, 'Your Turn To Wash The Stairs'. Mum had a rubber mat for kneeling on, a bristled scrubbing brush, a long bar of hard yellow soap, a very large cloth and a bucket of warm water to ensure that the stairs were spotless. Women took a pride in the standard of their stair cleanliness as they did with their whites on the washing line. An ointment or lotion would help to keep red washday hands at bay.
All families took their turn at lighting the stair gas lamps and if forgotten and it sometimes was, coming home from the cubs could be a daunting experience and one had to shout up at the window from the front street before entering the stair and hope mum or dad would come down to meet you.
A stair on a street was a close knit community and there was always a neighbour willing to call in to the family abode and check that all was well, do a double shift in washing the stairs, hang out the sheets or get the messages in if someone was sick or not feeling well. Perhaps it was the war time spirit lingering on.

Chapter 11- Soot And Fish

One day mum was bending over the fireplace stirring a large pot of broth when she let out a blood curdling scream. As we ran through from the big room she turned and dropped her hands from her face; we stood transfixed. She was black from her head, down the front of her peeny to her feet with soot which had fallen down from the inside of the chimney. Once we realised that she wasn't hurt, we burst out laughing and gave an impromptu performance of Al Jolson singing 'Mammy.'

It was time to call in the chimney sweep who duly arrived one Saturday morning with his long ladders and a multitude of brushes. His first task was to push into and spread around the fireplace a huge thick black sheet whilst another was hung from the mantelpiece to the base of the hearth. No fire had to be lit during the previous twenty four hours as per. the instructions from the sweep. Mum had already placed covers over as much of the furniture in the kitchen as possible to prevent dust from finding a clean surface to settle on.

'Right you children keep out of the kitchen,' Shouted mum.

'Och ma! We only want to see how the chimney gets swept.'

'Well just keep out of Jock's way.'

Outside the front door of the house, the ladders were placed into the hatch, high above the top landing which provided access for the sweep who climbed on to the roof to make the most important decision of the whole operation which was to identify the correct chimney pot to be swept out of the many standing in rows on the rooftop. Once the brush dropped down the chimney there was no going back and tons of soot would hurtle down into the hearth below and although mistakes did occasionally happen, it was the sweep's nightmare to get it wrong.

Jock's assistant a young lad called Tom who was waiting inside the kitchen, ducked under the corner of the long sheet, looked up the lum and waited for the shout from above.
'Sweeeeeeep!' was the cry down each chimney, from Jock. When the call went down the correct chimney, the response from Tom of 'that's me,' reverberated back up. If there was still any doubt about the identification of the correct chimney, the sweep would lower a rope down the individual lums until he felt two tugs from Tom which confirmed that sweeping could begin.
The sweep sent the large circular black brush with very stiff bristles down the chimney with a swishing sound, controlling the uncoiling rope until there was a dull thud of soot landing inside the sheet lying in the hearth.
'That's the first brush load,' said Tom to my mother.
The brush was hauled back up on the end of the rope. 'Stand by, sweeeeeeep!' came the cry again.
Swish, swish thud as the second load of soot fell.
Poking his head back under the sheet, Tom called up the lum 'Jock are you finished?'
'No, I'll do one more. Stand by, sweeeeeeep!'
Tom pushed and prodded various long handled brushes up the lum to loosen any soot still clinging to nooks and crannies and on a final inspection from the top down and the bottom up, the chimney was confirmed as swept. All that remained to be done was to remove the large sheet hanging in front of the hearth and gently shake all the soot into a central pile on the inner sheet, lying around the fireplace; trying to keep as much of the thick black dust as possible inside the hearth and out of the kitchen.
I was completely mesmerised by the heap of black soot and never did understand how Santa's beard could possibly stay so impeccably white. The outer sheet was thrown on top and all corners of the bottom sheet were thrown into the centre of the pile to envelop the huge black mound. The whole bundle was wrapped, tied together and carried downstairs with the ladders and brushes to the waiting van.
'I think that we just caught yer lum in time tae prevent it

gone up on fire Mrs Gee. There has been a number of chimney fires recently; too much soot, you've probably heard the fire engines around the streets,' said Jock on his return upstairs from the van.
'Aye,' said my mother, 'you wonder where it all comes from. Thank-you very much, it won't take me long to get the kitchen dusted, cleaned up and in ship shape again.'
'You'll no be needing me back for a wee while Mrs Gee. That'll be eight shillings please.'
Mum reached up to the mantelpiece where the money was ready and waiting to be paid out. 'Well worth every penny,' she said. 'I knew I was lucky to see a chimney sweep getting married the other day at St David's Church around the corner. He looked so smart in his old top hat, black tails and carrying his brushes over his shoulder. With his beautiful bride all in white, they made a lovely couple posing for their photograph. They got a big cheer from the crowd too. It fair brought a tear to my eye said my mother wiping the corner of her eye with the bottom of her peeny.
'Aye,' said Jock, 'we're good luck to have around weddings. Thanks Mrs Gee and good luck to you and your family.'
It wasn't long after that day when mum told us that there would be a surprise for us when we came home from school and there was. A new gas cooker had arrived. No more cooking over a coal fire, nor suffering from cold mornings as we dressed for school. We could now stand in front of the open oven door and let the heat waft around our bare legs and up our shivering bodies.
A gas ring on a long flexible lead attached to a pipe at the wall provided an extra outlet for boiling water or even cooking on whilst a gas poker was used to ignite the fire, saving whole boxes of matches.
Eventually electric light replaced the gas lamp in the house and in the stair. An old tea caddie was placed on the mantelpiece to save pennies and shilling pieces in readiness for the lights going out; sparking off unleashed panic to get money into the meter and allow light to sweep back into the room. A small clay pot on the mantelpiece held long spools made from thin strips of card which when

lit from the fire were used to light candles, cigarettes or even a pipe. Postcards, letters and knick knacks shared the space with numerous small household items where adult hands could reach them quickly and easily but were out of the way of meddlesome children. Two blue and white china Wally Dugs sat either side of the mantelpiece in their proper places surveying all that happened around the hearth and the comings and goings within the room.

I was now 10 years of age and old enough unofficially to take on a job delivering milk on weekday mornings before going to school.

The milk run was around St. Marys Cathedral in Palmerston Place and I had to report to Mr Nelson at his dairy by 7am. His list was amended daily according to customer's requests but he always had the long handled wooden barrow loaded with milk, rolls and bran scones checked and waiting for me. Rising early was a discipline that I retained throughout my life and when I joined the army, I had no difficulty in rising every morning at reveille albeit to the sound of the bagpipes. I was paid seven shillings and six pence for the delivery of which I gave my mother two shillings and six pence and was allowed to keep the rest as pocket money.

Buying fish for my mother one day at the local fishmonger in Morrison Street, the owner of the shop Sandy MacAlistair asked me if I would like a Saturday morning job. The pay would be three shillings plus a bacon roll with a cup of tea at break time.

I said 'Yes please,' if my dad would agree which he did.

My first task was to sweep the fish heads, tails and bones from the long slab in the back shop into a large wooden barrel and hose the slab down. The fish arrived early mornings from the various markets around Edinburgh. They were packed into long wooden boxes embedded in ice and were emptied on to the slab for Sandy to start gutting them with his razor sharp knives which I was well warned not to touch. Seeing the sticking plaster on a number of Sandy's nine fingers made me take the warning seriously.

Watching Sandy, I learned to dip my fingers into a bucket

of warm water to keep the circulation flowing when working around the slab. Wet dirty sawdust on the floor was swept up into the large dustbin and I had to replenish it with a sprinkling of clean fresh sawdust throughout the front and back shop. I would carry trays of fresh mackerel, cod, haddock, whiting, flounders and numerous varieties of large and small fish; herring, cod roe, kippers, smokies, fish cakes, live crabs and shellfish through to the front shop for Jill, Sandy's wife, to arrange and lay them out on the tiled counter which sloped down to the shop window, giving the customers an enticing view of the fresh harvests of the sea.
One morning Sandy asked me if I could ride a bike which I could but explained to him that I had never ridden a delivery bike with the large wicker basket on the front, especially an old rickety bike like the one in the back shop.
'Would you like to try a few deliveries Howard?' he asked. 'One or two customers are sick and can't make it into the shop. If you're willing to try, I'll raise your wages to five shillings.'
My eyes lit up, I smiled and said, 'yes thank- you. When do I start?'
'Now!' he said. 'Take the bike round to the lane in Torphican Street for a bit of practice.'
'The lane next to the police station?' I asked with some concern.
'Yes,' he replied, but don't wave or speak to any policemen you see and don't knock anyone over with the bike.'
'Right oh,' I said. 'Would you please lower the seat for me so that I can reach the peddles?'
After ten minutes and a couple of near misses against both walls of the lane, I was back at the shop anxious to get started with my first fish delivery and on a bike.
'Keep into the left hand side gutter,' Jill shouted, with a worried edge to her voice as I wobbled a bit leaving the shop with a couple of orders in the basket.
'Hi Howard. Gone yer sel.' I heard the voices as I passed some lads from the street but I didn't look up. 'Where did you get yer transport? At the dump by the looks of it.'
I ignored them gritted my teeth and decided to keep

concentrating on the traffic and think about my new pay rise. I cycled up Morrison Street, signalled right and turned into Gardeners Crescent before I had the confidence to relax and begin to look for stair numbers. Cycle clips kept my jeans off the oily chain and although I wore wellies in the shop I had put on my old boccles for cycling.
Fish scales stuck to my jeans like the sequins on a ballet dancer's tutu and when I pulled out a couple of bulging fish eyes from my pocket one day, my mother nearly had kittens. I immediately knew Sandy with his wild sense of humour had put them there. Finishing work, one Saturday lunchtime, as I turned the key in the door and walked into the house, I heard mum's voice. 'Is that you home Howard?'
'Yes mum. Did you hear me coming in?'
'No!' she said, 'I smelt you coming up the stairs.'
I was allowed from that week onwards to keep my full pay including my new rise which jingled in my pocket and I felt good. I now had a total income of twelve shillings and sixpence pence a week and mum decided on the amount to be saved and the amount that I could spend.
Ally, my younger brother wanted to get a job.

Chapter 12 - Two Narrow Escapes

It was a warm summer's day when Chipperfields Circus came to town and set up the Big top at Murrayfield next to the ice rink. Having paraded the elephants, horses, acrobats, clowns, bands and all the excitement of the circus along Princes Street everyone in Edinburgh knew that the circus had arrived. The big cats in their cages had gone straight to the showground to be fed and calmed down before the first show.

One Friday after school, Bobby, Rory, Wally and Albert had agreed to come home with me to persuade mum to allow me to go with them to the 4-30pm show which had a special rate of sixpence for children.

When mum saw the boys, she immediately looked at me and said, 'what are you lot up to?'

I thought it best to come straight out with it. 'Mum, can I please go to the circus this afternoon with my pals? I have been good all week, you said so yourself, only yesterday.'

'Well Howard,' began mum, 'Your dad and I had just been agreeing last night as to how hard you've been working and yes you can go to the circus but you'll have to change into your old clothes first and wear your jerkin; it'll be cold when you come out. I see that the boys have changed out of their school uniforms.'

'Oh great mum, thanks. I'll go and change right away. Can the boys wait in the big room?'

'Yes of course, I'll give you the entrance money and you can take your spending money from your savings; that will be enough for ice cream at the circus and chips at Roseburn on the way home,' said my mother planning it all out in her head. 'I presume that you are all walking there and getting a tramcar home. Have you boys got your entrance and spending money?'

'Yes, Mrs Gee,' they all answered together as if that's just

what they had been thinking about.
I made the quickest change ever and as we piled out the front door, I heard my mother's words of wisdom
'Just make sure that you keep out of mischief and watch that traffic at Haymarket'.
'Yes Mrs Gee we will. Bye! See you later,' was the cry as they bolted down the stairs.
'Thanks again mum,' I shouted and joined in the loud cheer as I hopped on to the banister and slid down to catch up with my pals, now waiting for me on the first landing.
From the top landing, I heard my mother's voice, 'get off that banister Howard.'
'Right ma,' I replied. 'Sorry.'
The show was fantastic and had all the thrills and spills promised on the huge posters pasted on walls throughout the town.
There was one act that really caught my imagination and that was the acrobats and tumblers who used trampolines to soar upwards towards the roof of the Big Top where they twisted and somersaulted before their feet pushed off again from the bed of the trampolines lifting them skywards above the applauding crowds.
The following Saturday when I got home, dad had gone to a pre-season match at Tynecastle and mum had gone to the washhouse taking Ally and Eleanor with her. I went into the wee room, jumped up on the double bed and started bouncing up and down, just as I had to seen the acrobats performing at the circus. Great fun! I was really good, I thought. It wasn't long before I was out of puff, took a breather and then decided that I was ready to rise in the world. I climbed up on the headboard of the bed, leaned against the wall and went for the full frontal somersault. I landed on the edge of the mattress and crashed on to the floor in a heap where I think, I lay for some time before I heard mum's voice.
'Howard, are you alright?' she asked as she crouched over me. 'What on earth have you been up to?'
My head was spinning. I was dizzy and faltered a little as she helped me slowly up on to my feet. I couldn't think straight nor even dare to attempt at explaining what I had

been trying to do.

'At least there are no broken bones,' mum said comfortingly. 'You can tell me all about it later. Come on through to the kitchen and have hot cup of sweet tea.'

I remember mum hugging me and giving me a cuddle which I did enjoy although I left that bit out when I related the story to my pals.

'You won't want to work in a circus then,' said Bobby.

I opened my mouth, scowled at him and said nothing.

Written homework was important and was corrected by the teacher the following day; usually accompanied by comments such as; Howard will have to improve, if he wishes to become an asset to the rest of society.

We were encouraged to work hard by our parents. Teachers had their own methods of dealing with disobedient and naughty children, utilising the tause which was a long piece of thick dark brown leather with a snake like tongue dividing into two at the end. The child to be punished would be called to the front of the class where all could have a clear view of the punishment about to take place. Nervously they would stand in front of the grinning teacher awaiting the inevitable instructions. 'Hold out your hand. Quite still now,' and the strap would be delivered downwards with force on to the palm of one's hand; sometimes leaving welts right up to and above the wrist. Quite often depending on the mood of the teacher, a double hander would be given out which meant the back of one hand was placed on to the palm of the other. The teacher would now feel conscience free to hold the belt with both hands above the shoulder and commence its downward sweep with impetus, generally accompanied by a sneering smile as leather struck flesh.

I have to admit to having more than my share of the belt at school but it was a better alternative than to being kept in after school or having to write 500 lines of e.g. I must behave and not upset my teacher who is a very busy person.

I never forgot the time that after being awarded a double hander from Miss Caruthers, I pulled my hands away before the belt reached my shaking palms. She lunged forward and struck her knees and legs with a mighty blow. She yelped and went scarlet, picked her glasses up off the floor, adjusted her drooping boobs beneath her floral smock and straightened the bun at the back of her hair. She looked me straight in the eyes, clenched her teeth and gave a twisted smile. The class erupted with laughter and shouted for an encore. I was mortified, rooted to the spot and could barely concentrate on the concise and clear instructions hissing from her mouth.

I was told to leave the classroom immediately and report to the head mistress in her office. 'Explain to her in precise detail why you have been given the belt,' said Miss Caruthers 'and why you have chosen to make a complete fool of your teacher in front of the class.'

I waited outside Miss Simond's office door for ages and ages listening to muffled voices inside. By the time the door opened and she came out with Wally Broon's mother, I had forgotten what I was to say to her.

'Well what is it boy?' she asked, the smile having left her face now that Mrs Brown was half way down the stairs and heading for the front door.

'I... I... I've been very silly miss and dropped the box of chalk all over the classroom floor but I've wiped it up and Miss Caruthers says that the janitor is not required but perhaps he would ask the cleaners to take a damp mop over it after school.'

She smiled, 'off you go now,' she said patting my head 'and thank- you for letting me know young man; that was very kind of you.'

I never heard another word about the matter but I did have a sleepless night. I think that it worked out well being a Friday afternoon and thus no school for a couple of days.

It was a narrow escape.

Chapter 13 - Woodcraft

On Tuesday night at the cubs, seven of us decided that on Saturday morning if the weather was dry, we would go to Corstorphine Woods to put into practise some of the woodcraft skills that we had been learning over the past few months. We agreed to meet at the big clock at Haymarket and take the tramcar out to the stop past the zoo. We would then walk up the hill, enter the woods and follow the track up to the tower which dominated the top of the hill.

We had decided to travel incognito and left our cub caps, green jerseys with badges sewn on and our yellow and brown neckerchiefs complete with woggles at home.

'Where are Callum and Albert?' I asked as we waited by the Hearts War Memorial at Haymarket watching the traffic whiz around the clock and shooting off in a number of directions.

'I don't think that they're coming,' said Titch Cameron. They got into some trouble yesterday; something to do with feeding a lost dog with pie and chips and then taking him to the police station where he was sick and had diarrhoea all over the floor in the front office. It turned out that the dog had been sitting outside the owner's door basking peacefully in the warm sunshine and hadn't been lost at all. Mrs Bruce the dog owner had been frantic with worry, calling for him and searching everywhere.'

'Oh well,' said Rory who was a Sixer in the pack, 'we'll just have to go without them.' We climbed on to the tramcar and made our way upstairs to the front family compartment.

'Hope you lot are not heading for trouble,' said the conductor eyeing up our small packs resting on our laps.

'Oh no,' we all said quickly in unison, looking around at each other for confirmation.

‘Where are you off to?’
‘We’re cubs.’ said Bobby Douglas; ‘on a training exercise.’
As we jumped off at our stop, the conductor leaned out of the tram and shouted, ‘have fun but watch out for the bears that have escaped from the zoo, they devour wee cubs for dinner.’
‘Is he kidding?’ asked Titch.
‘I think so,’ I said.
At the terminus the conductor hopped out and swung a long rope attached to an arm of an electric cable in an arc towards the rear of the tram, ensuring contact remained with the main electric power lines high above. Although I never really understood the technicalities that were going on, I knew that when the driver unbolted his tractor like seat and carried it through to the rear of the tram which now became the front, we could travel back in the direction it had just come from and we would get home safely.
We marched up the hill with Jimmy Brough leading the way. He was tall and gangly with long arms and legs to match and wearing his stout pair of walking boots he was able to stride out with ease and keep his pointed chin in front. With his tousled hair rifling in the morning breeze, his determined scowl and his woollen socks rolled down to his ankles, he looked ready to tackle Ben Nevis.
‘Slow down,’ said Titch, ‘I’ve only got wee legs.’
‘Aye,’ said Rory MacDougal, ‘I should be leading. I’m the Sixer of the Curlew Patrol you know’ but Jimmy kept going and started whistling as we reached the track at the edge of the woods.
‘See how many leaves we can identify and which trees they belong to,’ said Rory.
‘Why don’t we count the trees,’ was the facetious retort from Titch. Silence meant an all-round agreement.
Through the trees and up the track we marched behind Jimmy, making steady headway
‘There’s the tower,’ I shouted; pleased with myself that I had spotted it first ‘and there’s a wee dip next to that huge boulder where our fire would be sheltered.’ We sat down, took off our packs and decided to have something to eat and drink before lighting the fire and getting down to

serious cooking.
'Did we all bring some dough and a bottle of water?' I asked.
'Money?' asked Bobby scowling.
'No!! Flour to mix with water in our mess tins and roll into twists,' I shouted.
'Oh aye sorry,' mumbled Bobby, rummaging through his pack.
'Did you bring the matches Bobby?' asked Jimmy.
'Right here.' was the reply.
'Jimmy and I will get stones for the fire surrounds. Titch, you and Bobby collect twigs and dead wood. Rory, you try to find some long green sticks that won't burn when we toast the twists over the fire.'
Looking at me Rory paused and asked, 'how come you're making the decisions Howard? I'm the Sixer.'
'Well you decide what you want and delegate the duties to us,' I replied rather peeved.
'No it's alright. I'll go along with your arrangements. Let's get the fire going and I'll go and find some green twigs.'
With the fire underway, we mixed our flour and water rolling the effects into a long sausage like piece of dough which was then twisted thus the name, around each of our sticks. Allowing the leaping flames to die down, we held the sticks over the fire until the twists had turned brown and crusty; pure skill in our cooking, I thought to myself. When ready, we sat back hoping that they were edible and started to scoff them. The consensus of opinion was fantastic, really good, just right; delicious which was stretching matters a little too far. It was just as we sat back, so proud of our unsupervised cooking that we heard the voice.
'Hoi! You lot. There's no fires allowed in this wood.'
'Why not?' I asked. 'We're cooking our dinner.'
'That sign up there by the tower,' shouted the voice coming from an obvious irate man wearing plus fours, a tweed jacket and a matching cap; pointing upwards with his gnarled stick. 'It says no fires allowed.'
'We Cannae read it from here,' retorted Titch.
'Don't get cheekie with me,' he said whistling on his black

and white spaniel that was nosing into Rory's pack. 'I'll be reporting the lot of you to the Park Attendant when I pass his hut on the way down. Come on Digger,' he shouted as he strode past us scowling.

Digger, who now had his snout out of the pack took off down the hill with the last of Rory's sausage rolls hanging out of his dribbling mouth. Rory was mad and started shouting abuse at the dog when he suddenly remembered that he was a Sixer and should be controlling himself under all types of aggravation. He lifted a couple of fir cones and threw them half-heartedly in the direction of the disappearing stump of a wagging tail.

'We'd better get out of here,' suggested Bobby pushing mess tins, tin mug and jerkin into his pack. Taking the hint, we all started gathering up our survival bits and pieces.

'Don't forget the matches,' someone called out. 'Oh and the fire.'

'How will we put that out?' asked Jimmy, looking at the flames which had risen up again.

'Water,' I shouted.

'There's nae water left.' said Rory looking at me. 'Oh! I see.' He paused; 'a good idea. Right! Form a circle around the fire, this is an emergency.' called our leader.

'No!!' he shouted at Titch. 'Face inwards,' which we all did and suddenly everyone understood.

'Camp fires burning, camp fires burning,' sang Rory.

'Fetch water, fetch water,' we all joined in and we did.

'Aim straight boys,' shouted Bobby but too late; Titch squirted sideways and just missed me whilst Jimmy being taller scooted right over the flames and soaked Bobby. Rory making his own contribution didn't see where his waterfall had landed but the fire was doused and steam arose as we scattered the stones, grabbed our packs and took off down the hill.

As we turned a bend in the track, we ran straight into the path of the Wood Attendant wearing his dark blue uniform, peaked cap, welly boots and a scowl on his face; he looked quite formidable.

'Well what have you guilty looking boys been up to? Have you been trying to set my trees on fire?'

'Woodcraft.' answered Jimmy. 'We're cubs from the 152nd Gorgie Wolf Cub Pack.' I rolled my eyes in disbelief.
'There were some brownies up near the tower,' said Titch who received a nudge from Rory.
'152nd Pack you say? I know your cub master, Mr John Hewit. Please give him my best wishes; I'm Tom MacMurty.'
'We will, we will,' we echoed one another
'Hope you enjoyed your day out lads, perhaps there will be a few more badges being awarded soon. I'll walk on and catch those culprits lighting fires in my wood. Bye now. Best of luck with your Woodcraft Badge.'
'Bye sir,' we all shouted as we ran down through the trees to the road.
'What now?' I asked looking around our merry band.
'Why don't we go to the zoo?' suggested Jimmy.
'Any money?' I asked. Silence prevailed. 'Well that's that then,' I said.
After some moments of deep thinking; on the way home in the tram, Bobby asked, 'What's that man's name again?' Nobody could remember.
'I bet he spends the rest of the day looking for those troublesome brownies,' said Jimmy.
We all agreed that our experience had been good fun but we were not yet ready to put our names forward for the Woodcraft Test but as per our Cub Promise, we had done our best.
The following day the whole cub pack and scout group travelled by bus to Leith for an Open Day on HMS Vanguard. We were split into groups and members of the crew showed us around the ship. We were very impressed with the guns, the deck, the Captain's bridge, the canteen for meals and the long corridors and narrow staircases where we enjoyed running up and down pretending to be pirates. All of us suddenly wanted to be sailors and join the Royal Navy until we realised that not only were the toilets very impersonal with no doors but the small messing area where they ate their meals, read their books, harmonised and had their personal moments such as reading letters from home was also where they slept. Tables were made

down into bunk beds or in some areas, hammocks were slung on hooks from the ceiling. Storage for clothing was small chests and whatever tiny spaces were available behind water pipes. When someone mentioned rough seas and sea sickness, the army suddenly seemed quite appealing.
However we ate our packed lunches on deck and had a great day out. The sailors seemed a very happy and cheery bunch of lads who had taken us into their home and made us welcome. The next day the headlines of the local newspapers read that the Open Day had been a great success but the Vanguard was now sailing over the Forth to the breakers yard in Rosyth; now that its seaworthiness had come to an end.
We all felt a tinge of sadness for the rest of that day.

Chapter 14 - Boys Will Be Boys

Normal Practising School was an Episcopalian School in Orwell Place off Dalry Road. It was a small happy school and pupils had an inner pride in wearing the school blazer portraying the school badge and a navy blue and yellow tie. Although the playground was small it had an even smaller shelter for windy rainy days.

One Friday morning having had our bottle of milk we waited anxiously for the bell to ring to allow us to march down stairs and into the playground for the break. Walter Brown was casually collecting a haepenny from each of the boys.

The boy's and girl's toilets had one long continuous brick wall on the outside; ideal for throwing against and catching a rubber or tennis ball. On the inner wall, boys could often hear the girl's shared secrets by pressing their ears against a couple of hairline cracks but generally they had more important matters to attend to. The ventilation for both sets of toilets was provided by windows with metal bars fairly high up the wall. At playtime there was always a challenge amongst the boys to be first to reach the urinals inside which stood directly below the windows where the girls formed into their usual groups in the playground exchanging scraps ,skipping, standing around talking or playing with a ball.

The main competition was held on Friday mornings and the stakes were high. The winner was the boy who could pee the farthest up the wall, through the bars and out of the window. Although the entry fee was a haepenny one could have as many goes as time or the bladder allowed. Teachers often wondered why it was on a Friday that boys even in the winter preferred cold milk and didn't heat their bottles on the radiators as normal. With sixteen boys in the class eight pence was well worth trying for.

Mr Mitchell the janitor who suspected something was going on would storm up and down the playground between his other duties, determined to catch the guilty parties whatever they were guilty of but strategically placed lookouts would give the alarm on his approach and his short body and little fat legs were a definite asset to the success of the competition.

The first five boys would line up at the urinals, step back half a pace, aim at the windows and the competition was underway.

The skill lay in seeing who could not only pee the highest and furthest but in having the most accurate arc in guiding it through the bars. Some boys were really very good and it was suspected that they did practice.

One Friday morning there was suddenly high pitched screams from the girls outside. 'It's raining. It's in my hair.'

'Oh!!! We're soaked. It's from up there,' they shouted pointing at the toilet windows on the boy's side of the wall.

The janitor who had been prowling the playground came running into the boy's toilets. 'Right I've got you lot this time; at last you little monsters.'

Bobby Douglas had forgotten that he had agreed to be first lookout and had taken a place in the first line-up at the urinals.

'Who did it?' Mr Mitchell bellowed.

'Did what?' was the instant joint response.

'Urinated through those windows and on to the girls playing outside.'

'Not me,' came the joint response again.

'Right! All of you do your flys up now and come with me to the Headmistress's Office.'

We were herded over the playground like a flock of sheep. Children stopped playing and parted to make a passage for the condemned, to pass through.

'You dirty little beasts,' shouted Helen Mackay

'And filthy,' echoed Maggie Scott. 'It's all over our hair.'

'Aye!' yelled Wilma Craig. 'I washed it last night and I'll need to do it again tonight.'

'We'll tell our mothers. We know who did it,' shouted Helen Mackay who was dying to be involved in the action; 'wont

we Maggie?'
'It's a good job your mouth wasn't open,' retorted Donald Campbell.
'That's enough,' said the janitor as we reached the main school door. 'Get up the stairs and wait outside Miss Simond's office.'
Miss Simond was tall but slightly stooped at the hips. Her hair was short which emphasised the wrinkles across her forehead which in turn exaggerated her frown. When she spoke, she looked you in the eye and you knew she meant exactly what she said. She had been at the school for as long as anyone could remember and had hands like shovels which were sometimes used to smack the back of one's hand to save getting out her belt. Good manners and behaviour were important to her and the teachers seemed to enjoy her leadership qualities. Grown-ups were always asking in a kindly manner, if Miss Simond was still at the school. She was very much respected by parents and considered to be the pulsating heart of the school but pupils lived in fear of being sent to her office.
'Right!' said Miss Simond as we stood terrified in front of her desk. 'Mr Mitchell tells me that you have been doing wicked things. Is that correct?'
Heads shook from side to side as we all denied the charge. Miss Simond closed her left eye, cocked her head and looked along the line from right to left where Mac was standing sniffing with a runny nose.
'We'll start with you Macdonald. What have you to say for yourself?'
'It wisnae me Miss. I wisnae needin and I couldnae pee.'
'You mean urinate,' she interrupted.
'I even tried whistling and waving it around with my fingers.'
'Alright! Alright! Do spare me the details, but you did try?'
'Yes miss,' he said sheepishly.
'Donald Campbell; what's your story?'
'I only got halfway up the wall Miss. I didn't even reach the window-sill before I saw it running back down.'
'Hmm!' muttered Miss Simond. 'I cannot believe that I'm hearing this.'
'Howard Gee, do tell me.'

'It wasn't me Miss.'
'Were you not involved in some kind of trouble a few weeks ago?'
'Oh no Miss, I was off sick that day when the janitor's bike went missing. Mr Mitchell thought that it was me running away with the bike but he had just made a mistake.'
'And are you better now?'
'Err! I think; I think so Miss.'
'Well you are guilty this time are you not?'
'Oh no Miss,' I said, 'my arc of pee, err. sorry urination'
'Urine,' she interrupted.
'Isn't high enough to reach the bars and I could only nearly reach them,' I continued.
She shook her head, said nothing and rolled her eyes heavenwards as if praying for patience and divine guidance.
'Right Douglas your turn, speak.'
'It wisnae me either Miss, I was bursting but couldnae get my buttons opened quickly enough and I wet my pants. Look Miss, I dribbled down my trouser leg and my school socks and shoes are soaking. I've never had this problem before Miss.'
'I don't wish to see thank you,' she retorted indignantly, 'but I note that the result might have been different had you been in control of your bladder and that you have been involved in this foul act before.'
'Walter BROWN, your turn; do explain.'
'It wisnae me Miss.'
'Why? Do tell.'
'Well my willie is just no big enough. I can't even hold it with two hands and I've never won the kitty Miss.' There was a pause:
'Kitty! Kitty? What do you mean kitty?. Tell me now!!'
'Oh Broon!' We all mumbled together.
'Quiet! Let Brown explain for himself.'
'Oh well you see Miss, we, that is all the boys in the class put a haepenny into a kitty and the winner who pees best through the bars collects the money.'
'Oh do they!' exclaimed Miss Simond.
'Well sometimes Miss, there has to be a pee off, oh! sorry

Miss, I mean a urination off.'
'You mean to say that there is gambling going on over this foul deed?' asked Miss Simond fighting hard to control her emotions and blood pressure.
'Right I've heard enough. As with immediate effect this foul action has ceased.'
'You will each receive one double hander of the belt from me now and I will give you a letter to take home to your parents.'
As we left the office we heard Miss Simond's voice behind us; 'now let that be a lesson to you all' but as her door was closing I thought I heard her mutter to herself, 'I don't believe it.'
'Oh that wis sair,' said Bobby.
'Aye!' We all agreed blowing into our hands.
'Walter just give everybody back their entry fee,' I said as we made our way downstairs and back into the playground where we burst into fits of laughter.
Somehow the letters to our parents got lost on the way home.

Chapter 15 - In Trouble Again

The word in the playground was that the pet shop at Haymarket had tortoises in stock and a crowd of us boys decided to go and see them during the school dinner break. After our third warning not to touch the tortoises that were creeping around a large pen we were thrown out of the shop.

With a quick glance left and right, we ran over the road to the bakers where we bought pies and walked back up Dalry Road past the fruit and veg. shop and on to the Scotia Cinema where John Wayne was starring in Fort Apache. As we crossed back over the road to the school in Orwell Place someone spotted movement inside Corky Parker's jerkin. We couldn't believe our eyes when he pulled out a tortoise.

'Did you buy that?' asked Donald. 'How much was it?'

'I didn't buy it,' retorted Corky. 'It's just in there to keep warm. I borrowed it to give to Kenny the wee lad that lives below me in my stair. He was born with a hole in his heart and can't run and play as we can. He doesn't get out very much. His mother has told him that if she could have afforded it, she would have bought him a budgie.'

'Where's his dad?' asked Titch Cameron.

'He didn't come home from the war,' replied Corky.

'You'll need a box,' I said.

'I've got one. It's an old apple box and it's lying in our back green. I'll run home now, put it in the box, leave it in my house and give it to Kenny before my mother gets in at 5o'clock.'

'Have you got any food or water for it?' I asked and before I could say, that the school bell would be ringing in a minute, Rory MacDougal produced a large lettuce from under his jumper.

'He can have this,' he said.

'Did you take that from the fruit and vegetable display at the front of Smith's window?' I asked.
'I heard the shop assistant say as we passed, if you've not got any food for that poor wee tortoise, just help yourself to a lettuce and I did.'
'We can't go around stealing. Give it here,' I said. 'I'll take it back and tell her that it had been lying on the pavement and ask if she would let us have it for what's his name again?'
'He hasn't got one yet.' Corky answered.
'That's the bell ringing now,' someone shouted.
'Right,' I shouted, grabbed the lettuce and dashed back across the road to the shop and that's when it happened.
I never saw the tramcar and when I opened my eyes, a very worried driver and conductor were looking down at me with a sea of faces around them.
'Are you alright son? Your leg is bleeding a wee bit. Can you move it?'
'Aye, I'm fine,' I said as I stood up, spying the remains of a squashed lettuce under the front of the tram; wondering if it was a tortoise. The driver took my name and address and Miss Murray a teacher from the school who had been at the nearby post office told him that she would look after me and take me back to school.
Assuring the driver that I was okay, I said, sorry for causing such a commotion and thanked him for saving my life. I was accompanied back to school by the gang and Miss Murray with her arm around my shoulders and my cheeks the colour of Robert Burns' Red, Red Rose. At the school, she bathed my leg with warm water and dettol, wrapped a bandage around it and took me to the Headmistress's office.
'What have you been up to now young Gee?' Miss Simond asked, having already had the gist of the story from the policeman standing in her office. She gave me a hug before telling me that the policeman wanted to ask me some questions about the accident and record the relevant details in his notebook.
He spoke quietly but firmly and assured me that I was a very lucky lad and it all could have been more serious. It

was thanks to the quick reaction of the driver that he had been able to stop the tramcar in time, allowing me to be standing here today.
'Yes sir.' I said.
On completion of his report, a few words passed between him and Miss Simond and as he left the office he smiled at me and in a kindly voice said; 'glad you're alright son, just be careful crossing the road in future.'
Miss Simond gave me a note for my father and explained to me that running around head down, not looking where I was going was never a wise thing to do. 'You may have heard the story about the hare and tortoise,' she said.
I blinked. 'Yes Miss.'
'Well let that be a lesson to you in future.'
'Yes Miss.'
At three thirty that afternoon when the bell went and the school doors opened, I was surrounded by pupils and was the hero of the day. I decided to chum Corky home and make sure that after all the excitement, the tortoise was cared for.
In Corky's back green we retrieved the wooden box and filled it with some dried grass, a piece of apple ,half a tomato, a small carton of water and headed upstairs to Kenny's door on the first landing. As we climbed the stairs, we met old Mrs Gray wearing her headscarf and welly boots coming down the stairs en route to the shops. Two empty message bags hung from her left arm as she peered inside the box.
'What's that?' she asked.
'It's a tortoise Mrs Gray,' Corky answered.
'Where did it come from?'
'Africa,' I said.
'That's a long way,' she muttered.
'I know,' said Corky. It must have taken it ages; it's a really slow walker.'
'Don't be cheeky,' she said, scowling at the two of us. 'I'll be telling your mother.'
My mother knows a tortoise walks slowly,' Corky replied as we rushed past her and up the stair to Kenny's house. That afternoon one little boy was very happy and promised that

he would look after his new pet.
Somehow our good deed seemed to override the fact that the tortoise hadn't been paid for.
Kenny said that he would call it Curly.
One day word got around that two older boys who had recently left the school had been up in court for breaking into shops and stealing sweets and cigarettes amongst other things. They had been found guilty and sent to borstal for two years. We were stunned and shocked.
My mother fussed over me when she read Miss Simond's letter about my accident. I suppose I did play on it for a few days.
My dad suspected that there was more to it than met the eye and warned me about the dangers of crossing roads when my mind was on other matters, 'and keep out of mischief,' he called; which were his last words on the matter.
The following week a policeman arrived at the door to inform my mother that I had been identified as the guilty boy who had thrown a stone from the back green through Mrs Trayner's window. It had landed in a pot of hot soup which was cooling at the sink. Whilst no one had been hurt, the soup had splashed all over her kitchen wall and left her without a meal that evening not to mention the cost of replacing the window pane. The fact that it had been snowing heavily that morning and we had been sledging, making a giant snowman and rolling in the snow which developed into a huge snowball fight, was no excuse for me unwittingly scooping up a stone with my snowball. Matters were only made worse by my pathetic aim at Billy Macleod and hitting the window. It also seemed that I made a rude gesture at MrsTrayner when she appeared angrily at the window before I took off. I couldn't remember that bit but she was positive that Billy Macleod was with me.
Mum agreed to pay the cost of replacing the pane of glass out of my pocket money and to deal with the culprit; me. Oh dear, in trouble again. I was marched down to MrsTrayner and made to apologise for the trouble and the worry that I had caused her.

.‘Don’t worry son,’ she said, ‘we were all young once, even if it was a long time ago.’
I shook my head and smiled. ‘Sorry,’ I said again.
Mum told me that Mrs Trayner who lived on her own, was nearly seventy years of age and didn’t need any unnecessary worries. Later that week I went round to her house with a basket of tatties, carrots, onions, a leek and a ham shank ,compliments of dad. She said that she would make a lovely pot of lentil soup which would last for days.
She thanked me very much and said what a nice boy I was. I enjoyed the stick of Edinburgh Rock that she put in my hand as I left her at the door. She smiled and waved.
That evening as I got ready for bed, I felt good.

Chapter 16 - Fun And Games

The stair was our beating heart of life and the street was its artery.
Boys played on the front street at hide and seek, chasey, football, bools, conkers and a myriad of games. Rubber car tyres were collected from the dump at Russell Road near Tynecastle, home of the Hearts Football Club and rolled home using a stick to control the direction of travel. We swapped cigarette cards and comics of film stars, football players, cowboy and war heroes not to mention Superman, Spiderman and Captain Marvel. Guiders were homemade from wooden boxes to which we fitted old pram wheels with rubber tyres or ball bearing wheels attained from Asa Wass the rag merchant at the top of the street in exchange for any kind of old clothes or even just rags. Although football could be played in the back greens, families had different allotted days for hanging out their washing and it was a very brave boy who kicked a muddy ball when white sheets, towels and nappies were on the drying lines; then we just played in the street.
Footballs had a leather outer cover containing an inner rubber bladder which required a strong pair of lungs to blow it up and if one's forehead when heading the ball, caught the lace on the front of the cover, one's eyes watered for some moments.
Making tattie boggles was a popular pastime. Used matchsticks were pushed into large tatties creating a hedgehog effect which were then rolled down the stairs or the street under 'international rules', to see whose boggle reached the nominated finish line first.
At week-ends with a couple of older boys leading the way, we cycled to Corstorphine Woods, Gullane and even to Dunfermline Abbey crossing the Forth by the St. Margaret's Ferry at South Queensferry. With a bike,

children had almost unlimited freedom to wander and explore although I suppose mothers did worry at times but knew that there was safety in numbers although the rules at home did stipulate explaining where the destination was and the approximate time of return. We were taught how to use a public telephone, in the event of an emergency as long as we could find one and had a few pennies in our pocket.
Girls played ball games against the wall, sang ditties to accompany their skipping, chalked up pavements for their peevery beds, exchanged scraps, played shops, dressed up as nurses and played with their dolls and prams. Sometimes they would hang about discussing their favourite film stars, talking secrets, smirking and giggling or even just following boys around and generally being a nuisance.
Sometimes boys would let girls play with them at rounders, dodge ball, hide and seek ,peeries and whips, kick the can and concerts; ringing doorbell and running away although that wasn't really a game; just fun.
Families took their turn in sweeping, washing and cleaning the stair whilst polishing and shining the brass bells which stood in vertical rows either side of the outside stair door facing into the street. A deep pride was taken in the standard of cleanliness of the bells and the stairs.
From the railway bridge downhill to the fruit and veg. shop on the corner, time trials with guiders were popular with us children but not with mums coming up the hill, carrying messages or pushing prams nor with the old folks whose reactions to side stepping were not as sharp as they had been in days gone by.
Winter meant snowball fights, building snowmen, sledging and clearing doorways and paths. Sometimes, if we were lucky, we would be given a couple of pennies or even a three penny piece from someone who remembered their own childhood days of clearing snow.
Easter meant rolling eggs at the Blackfords or Arthurs Seat not to mention delicious chocolate eggs bought from Jenny Halloways who sold every kind of sweets and chocolates available including sugar mice, puff candy, gobstoppers,

sherbet dabs, chocolate ice lollies, sticks of liquorice and bars of cream and chocolate toffee. When sweets came off the ration after the war, Jenny's was a very popular shop, especially with children.

When children were having fun, it was always very difficult to get them to come in for their meals or especially for bed. It was common for mums to hang out of windows calling to their children playing in the street below.

'Come up now, yer teas ready.'

'Can I have a wee while longer ma please?' would be the standard response.

'Quarter of an hour then,' my mother would often shout back and bargaining had begun.

'Half an hour ma, please.'

'Twenty minutes and that's your lot.'

'Thanks ma. I'm hungry; could I have a piece on jam please to keep me going?'

'You'll never eat yer tea'

'I will ma, honest. Please, please.'

After a couple of minutes, the top floor window would open again and mum would lean out with a piece on jam inside a paper bag which she would throw, usually with spot on accuracy to land on the pavement at my feet. On one occasion she missed the target, the bag caught on the iron railings, tore open and the jam piece landed in the basement directly below our top flat window. I had promised to share it with my pal Jimmy who had shared his with me the night before.

We pushed open the iron gate of the basement, and ran down the steps to find the piece lying in the middle of a huge dog poo. 'Au crivvens,' I muttered. We were horrified, looked at each other and ran back up the stairs to review the situation.

Between us we had five pence left from the wedding pooroot the previous Saturday morning and ran up the road to Mary's, the chip shop where we bought and shared a threepenny bag of chips with salt, sauce and vinegar and still had a penny each left.

Chapter 17 - Folk Around The Street

Word quickly got around if someone in the street was getting married as it meant a pooroot. The taxis would arrive and it didn't matter whether it was the Bride, Groom, Best Man or Best Maid mums or dads, the windows of the taxies were wound down on the pavement side and halfpennies, pennies and threepenny bits were thrown and scattered on to the pavement for the children crowding round. One of the better ideas of marriage was a pooroot.

Confetti was everywhere but Joey the scaffe was never far behind, sweeping pavements and gutters with his long handled broom made up from bundles of twigs bound together to form a brush head. Cigarette ends and general rubbish would be methodically swept up into his trusty shovel and deposited into his metal barrow which had two lids, two large rubber wheels, and a conglomerate of bags not to mention bits and pieces hanging from it. His large gloves, if not being worn would stick out from beneath one of the lids.

Joey was a chirpy character with a dark scar running down the left side of his neck which had been the result of an illness when he was young, so he said. He didn't have a uniform but always wore an old army battledress top with a pair of ex. army ammunition boots complete with metal studs on the soles. His hair was kept in place by a wee grey bunnet, tipped to one side and balanced precariously on his head. As he whistled and hummed to himself, he went up and down the streets sweeping and shovelling litter into his barrow. One New Year when he had consumed a dram or two or three, a picture is conjured up of him half asleep, cross legged, propped up by his barrow with a cigarette dangling from his mouth; it was a memory to cherish.

Like Joey, Frankie the milkman was known by everyone

and he didn't need any encouragement to stop for a blether. They were both small and stocky like two book ends and they seemed to meet most mornings at the steps of our tenement. After the woodbines were lit, the serious business began. A newspaper and a pencil were pulled out from a pocket and a short discussion would take place before a piece of paper had the name of a horse scribbled on it. Money was passed from one to the other prior to being taken with the betting slip to Jimmy Macpherson, the bookies runner who depending on the start times and venues of the daily horse racing, would turn up outside the Royal Antediluvian Order Of Buffaloes Club on the opposite side of the street near the pigs bins and the lamp post. No real names were ever written on the betting slips which were always signed with a nom de plume at the bottom right hand corner. Sometimes the runners would be carrying a lot of money in the inside pocket of their jacket or coat and were a tempting target for any skulking rogues but they were street wise and regularly changed their times and routes when taking and handing over cash to their bookies. At the end of the day when races had been run and won they would be back on their pitch paying out winnings to the lucky punters. Every now and again they would be arrested, taken to the cells at the Police Headquarters on the High Street which always upset their planned routine for that day. After a few hours, they would be released but later in the month they would have to go to court, charged with illegal activities and have to pay a fine which the bookies themselves would pay for them.
Legal Betting shops altered the whole betting system and eventually when television arrived ordinary people could watch the races in comfort as they were run.
'Ah well!' such was the progression of life and its changing ways which were indeed often a mystery but few could have foreseen the European way of life creeping in even when Onion Johnny cycled around the streets with his bicycle laden with strings of onions.
As each door opened to his knock he would respond with 'Bonjour Madame, I am here from sunny France especially to bring you my very best onions.'

'Hello Johnny. I haven't seen you for a while,' was often the response.
'Well no,' he would say, 'I have been waiting for my onions to ripen to perfection. Sil vous plait, you buy?' he would say holding out a string of large onions. 'You touch, you feel, they are fresh and ripe and very heavy for me to peddle on my bike.' With his black beret, dark moustache sun tanned features, red and black jersey, his accent and natural French charm; housewives had no chance of refusing. They fell under his spell, bought his onions and hung them on the kitchen door handle until a more suitable storing place could be found.
I always thought that it was a long way to cycle back to France for the next load of onions and never did work out how Johnny did it.
'Thank- you for calling Johnny.'
'Merci, merci and au revoir,' he would call with a broad smile stretching across his face as he looked over his shoulder and gave a farewell wave of his hand.
'Ah!!,' was the gentle sigh heard up and down the street as Johnny passed by.
When the cobbles on the street were being replaced, holes being filled in or drainage pipes being renewed; security ropes and danger signs would be set up. At night, old Bill the watchman would come on site to ensure the safekeeping of machines, working tools, equipment and stores including the coke for his fire. He had to have eyes in the back of his head to ensure that children didn't crawl under the barriers, trip and fall down holes nor walk home with a bucket of the precious coke.
Outside Bill's wee sentry box was a brazier with a welcoming warm glowing fire from the burning embers of the coke. He was happy for us to stand around the fire whilst he drunk his hot sweet tea from his tin mug. One evening, he told us that his wife had died, his family were scattered up and down the country and that he didn't see them very often. He spoke quietly and had a sad lonely expression on his face.
It was a Friday night when he told us that he had something special for us and from his hut he lifted out a

bag of chestnuts which we roasted on his fire and sat listening to his stories from his long and what seemed an exciting life. It was getting dark but as there was no school in the morning, we had been allowed to stay up a little later than usual. Eventually we heard the cries of our mothers, 'it's time for bed, come on up the stairs now.'

'One more story Bill please,' we all shouted together.

'No, No,' he said, 'its bedtime, your mothers are calling you up the stair; off you go now; I'll have another story for you tomorrow.'

'Thanks Bill,' we all cried as we left him, pulling his bunnet down over his head, his collar up and his scarf tightly around his neck. Grasping his mug of hot tea with two shaking hands, he nodded to us as we left the fire and headed home. It was a cold, bitter night.

'See you tomorrow Bill. Thanks for the stories.'

'I enjoyed telling them to you,' he shouted back. 'Don't forget to say your prayers and say one for me.'

At breakfast the following morning, mum told us that old Bill had passed away in his sleep beside his fire. We couldn't quite take it in and felt very sad as we sat in silence on the front steps of the tenement.

We never did get that other story.

Chapter 18 - Doos And Horses

I had promised Ranald Bains who lived across the street from me that I would help him clean out his big brother's dookit which was a large wooden shed in his back garden where Ian kept his prize pigeons. Ian's doos or pigeons were his pride and joy and he was known locally for his quality of birds. His horseman had won a number of prizes and when it took to the skies, pouted his cheeks, pushed out his chest and performed a couple of acrobatic swoops the other pigeons just swooned and followed him back into the dookit. Ian would then sell them back to their owners, identified by the registered number, stamped on the ring which was fitted around one leg of the bird. At the weekly doo market the price of purchasing a new bird or buying back your own depended on the quality of the bird, the number of races it had won and on the skill of haggling between the seller and the buyer. It was all standard procedure, accepted by the doo men of Edinburgh.
Ranald hadn't told his brother of our cleaning out plan but had hoped to surprise him and get some extra pocket money which he would share with me. Having ensured that the main door and the windows leading to the outside landing platform were closed and bolted from the inside; at least we thought they were, we had just started cleaning the floors of the internal cages when suddenly the door flung open and Jimmy Brough entered. 'Do you want a hand?' he asked with a large smile on his face.
"Close that door now!' screamed Ranald.
'What's up?'
In a flash, the pride of the dookit flew out the door followed by a horde of other birds who glimpsed freedom and took off up into the clear blue sky. We looked at each other and didn't know whether to cry, murder Jimmy or throw our arms in the air and stamp our feet but after grabbing the

door and slamming it shut, we chose the latter.
Jimmy who couldn't understand why the door was not locked scowled and shouted back, 'you didnae hae the 'keep out' sign up; Ian always has it up when he's cleaning the dookit. Does he know you two are in here?'
'It's none of your business;' shouted Ranald, 'now get lost.'
'There's the sign hanging on the nail in the corner. I'll put it up on the outside of the door as I close it on the way out,' said Jimmy sarcastically. 'I hope that Ian's homers had their maps with them and that he doesn't count the ones that are left when he gets home tonight,' he shouted over his right shoulder as he left, accompanied by our mumblings and rude gestures.
After two hours of looking up at the sky, our necks were beginning to creak when the horseman suddenly appeared above the chimney tops, circled around and flew down on to the landing platform of the dookit. Eventually we were able to bribe it in with some very tempting quality pigeon maize. Two or three fantails followed and were quickly locked up before Ranald's brother came home. Others must have decided to leave home or were taken in by one of Ian's competitors. I remember thinking at the time, that for quality homing pigeons, they couldn't have been very well trained or they wouldn't have got lost.
I kept out of Ian's way for at least a couple of weeks.
Ranald got no pocket money that week and was not allowed out to play for five days. Ian went about snarling, growling and threatening a slow death if we ever again went anywhere near his birds. We didn't have the courage and thought it probably better not to ask for some remuneration for the work that we had carried out.
Frankie the milkman was promoted from pushing a barrow containing bottles of milk to being in charge of a horse and cart. In shirt sleeves his arm muscles could be seen bulging which was a direct result of him pushing his barrow around the streets including up and down Grove Street. He always wore a Hib's green and white woolly hat with a matching pom-pom which could be seen bobbing up and down the stairs during his deliveries. He was good at his job and the milk generally got delivered on time; leaving

outside each door the required amount of milk according to the number of tokens left with the empty milk bottles. He was usually grateful for assistance from us children who thought nothing of darting up to the top flats carrying his bottles of milk for him.

'Don't drop them,' he would shout, 'or you'll get no wages.'

'You don't give us any wages.' we replied

'Don't worry about details,' he would say, 'concentrate on getting up those stairs and delivering the milk without dropping and breaking the bottles; folk are waiting to start their breakfast.

As the carts were kept at St. Cuthbert's Yard in Morrison Street, the horses were taken down Grove Street in pairs from the stables to the yard in the very early hours of the morning. They were hitched up to the shafts of the carts which were already loaded with crates of milk by the night shift staff and the milkmen would then head off on their normal rounds throughout Edinburgh. The rounds having been completed, the horses were then walked back up Grove Street to the stables about twelve mid-day to be watered, fed, groomed and rested in readiness to start the morning rounds all over again.

Further up the street, the huge brewery horses pulling and straining at their reins, hauling their drays full of barrels of beer were a magnificent example of working horses delivering to pubs around Edinburgh from the brewery at Fountainbridge. Huge bundles of sacking filled with straw protected the pavements from the heavy barrels which were rolled off the carts. The sand bins located at the top of the street near the railway bridge were a necessity on wintry days for sanding the icy, slippery cobbles, assisting the wheels to grip the road especially going downhill. Large shovels were always carried on the drays to allow the carters to shovel and spread the sand on to the road as required.

Nose bags full of hay and a bucket to fill with water for the horses swung on hooks under the carts. On special occasions such as Gala Days and weddings, ceremonial coaches would be rolled out from under their wraps. Horse brasses were buffed until gleaming, harnesses and reins were polished whilst manes and tails were platted with coloured ribbons and trimmings portraying a deep pride in the horses by their individual carters. The horses knew when it was a special day; perhaps it was the time spent on the brushing, the patting, the fussing and talking quietly in their ears not to mention that extra apple or two that gave the game away. They knew that the next day they would be back delivering their heavy loads to the waiting customers.

As the carts went up and down the street, we would sit passively and innocently on the front steps of the tenement until the moment that we were out of sight of the carter's eyes. Judging the time to be right, we would leap up, grab the back of the cart, hold on and run as fast as our legs would go until we could pull ourselves up to sit on the back for a free ride. If the horse happened to perform an act of nature whilst running behind the cart, we could only hold on and run through the usually very large puddle or even worse if we saw the tail being lifted, we knew what was coming but couldn't do a thing about it. Holding on even tighter, our shoes slipped on the cobbles which were splattered with the endless flow of natural waste erupting from the rear end of the horse.

A cold water tap, just inside the nearby coal depot allowed us to wash our shoes and socks on the way home whilst agreeing on the story to tell our mothers about our wet feet.

It was great fun and we would laugh all the way home.

It was our street and we were growing up happy.

Chapter 19 - Deliveries And Communications

The pavements and roads were always under repair and one day a number of manhole covers on the pavement had been lifted, inspected, readjusted, closed and resealed around the joints with fresh putty. To us children, putty was a magical play substance that could be squashed, bent and crafted into numerous objects such as figures and animals. Games with putty were invented and when squeezed in one's hand it made one feel good. It was similar to plasticine but from a source free of charge.

No sooner had the workman gone back around the corner at the bottom of the street when we set to work digging out the putty. The following morning fresh putty sealed the covers again and a warning notice 'Danger Keep Off' had been erected.

As we sat quietly on the steps watching the world go by, we saw the red faced irate workman coming towards us.

'Did you kids remove that putty yesterday?' he snarled.

'Na,' we answered. 'No us.'

'Well who did then?'

'We dinae ken mister but it wisnae us,' answered Billy Macleod on behalf of us all

'We saw some bigger boys from Brandfield Street,' said Ewan one of the twins pointing his chin in that direction up the hill. 'They were poking about,' I said.

'Well you tell them that if I catch them, they'll get the toe of my right boot up their rear ends.'

'We'll tell them.' we all said nodding our heads in agreement.

'Aye right,' he said as he turned and walked away mumbling to himself and looking over his shoulder at us.

We gave him a good five minutes before we tackled the first two manholes when would you believe it, who comes back around the corner with steam coming out of his ears; only him. He was pointing; shaking his fist and shouting swear words in an unmistakable very angry manner. What else could we do but take-off up the front steps of the tenement and straight down the back stairs; past the bogey holes and into the back green where the escape routes awaited. We scattered; over walls, between railings and through lines full of washing including sheets and pillow cases. We ran through smaller greens and headed for the escape routes via other back green doors; thinking out Plan B in case they were locked. Through dark passageways, dodging green-eyed black cats until we emerged into the freedom of a number of surrounding streets where we met up puffing and out of breath but free to think again.

'Phew!' A narrow escape; not caught; no parental punishment although as he left for work next morning, dad looked at me with his head shaking slightly as if to doubt my answer before the question was asked.

'I heard about some bother on the front street yesterday. I hope that you weren't involved. Were you?'

'Me?' I asked

'Yes you.'

'Not me dad but I'll try to find out what happened and who was involved.'

He ignored me, collected his daily piece which was today a slice of porridge. Mum had prepared it the previous night, left it in a drawer to thicken up before cutting it into slices along with a large piece of potted haugh.

I shook my head as he went out the door. 'Why am I always suspected of being part of any trouble that occurs in this street?' I asked myself. I thought loud enough for dad to know what I was thinking but he wasn't even listening and didn't bother to stop and reply.

When the coal horse and cart arrived in the street, children knew to keep well out of the way of the coalmen who swung the one hundredweight bags of coal off the cart, on to their backs, climbed the stairs around tight corners and

strode into the waiting houses on various levels. They couldn't look down, stop, nor swerve for small children playing or for any toys left on the stairs. Usually, they wore black caps with shiny leather tops and huge ex-army sleeveless jackets as worn by drivers of army vehicles. Their shirt sleeves were rolled up showing off tattoos of their mothers and loved ones. Some were rather shocking on their forearms and chests and would remain with them for the rest of their lives as souvenirs from their war service and drinking nights out. Their shirts attracted daily grime and dust and had to be washed and mended regularly but they always seemed to take a pride in their work and be turned out fresh and ready to tackle the day's work with a smile. Dark trousers were often held up by braces and a broad leather belt helping to support their backs which needed all the help they could get. A strong pair of sturdy boots supporting the ankles and gripping the stairs were a must. Padding on the back of the neck and shoulders helped to prevent chaffing by the inevitable moving bags. With black faces and hands they often looked like cotton pickers from the Deep South as described in Mark Twain's stories of Tom Sawyer and Huckleberry Finn.
The coal was tipped into the coal bunker in front of the kitchen window releasing dust and stoor everywhere; usually just when mum had cleaned, polished and dusted throughout. The bunker stored the hammer for breaking the large lumps of coal, firewood, axe, firelighters and a brush and shovel. When the lid was closed, three children could sit on it comfortably.
One evening when Ally my brother and I were kneeling on it, pushing and shoving for the best view of the horses coming down from the stables en route to the Tattoo, my head went through a pane of glass. I received a cut above my left eye but was fine after the doctor sewed in two stitches although I couldn't head a football for a couple of weeks.
All houses had the wireless which required accumulators to do the work of batteries. They were exchanged on a regular basis at the dry-salter's shop for a small sum of money.

Coalmen, milkmen and postmen were an important ready source of news and information; and were always glad of a breather and a blether.
Sporting their navy blue jacket, Royal Mail badge and the famous blue cap, postman would stride up and down the stairs with their sacks of mail, bundles of letters tied up with rough string and various small parcels often whistling the latest tunes to help them shut out the effort of climbing the stairs.
Telegrams were delivered by a young lad on a bike and wearing a bell boy hat with the leather strap under his chin. His dark blue tunic was tight fitting and bicycle clips kept the bottoms of his trousers from catching the oil dripping off the chain. The arrival of a telegram immediately raised a sense of excitement but was a real dread and fear during the war years as it often meant the delivery of bad news.
The bell would be rung, the door would be opened, a cursory glance at the contents of the telegram and a smile, a look of despair or a tear would say it all.
'Any reply Ma'm? The telegram boy would ask.

Chapter 20 - Community Spirit

Dustbin men emptied the buckets which were left on the edge of the pavements by families the night before their allocated collection days. Ashes went into a metal bin, general rubbish into another and tattie peelings and vegetable matter were taken over the road to be tipped into the pig's bins which were emptied regularly by a farmer in a large blue lorry, driven in from the outskirts of town.
Like the milkman, postman, scaffe and coalman, the dustbin men carried out their tasks in hail, rain, sleet or shine usually with a smile. They were given a tip at Christmas and a dram of whisky at New Year respectively. How they ever finished their rounds, got their horses back to the stables and themselves home before collapsing in a heap was a real mystery but somehow life rolled on.
Mr and Mrs Michael and family who lived opposite our tenement had an upmarket bed and breakfast catering for show business personalities and from our top flat window we could watch the taxies coming and going. One morning there were newspaper reporters and photographers causing quite a stir outside their house, waiting on the arrival of a well known singer who had just released a huge hit with 'The Finger of Suspicion Points At You.' It was Dickie Valantine; a singing sensation who was especially popular with the girls.
Sometimes Mrs Michael would invite mum, Ally, Eleanor and me over for afternoon tea into their small, private back garden which had a lawn surrounded by flowers. They had two children who went to private school and were a very nice family although I think a bit posh.
On washday, the pavement was a hive of activity with an assortment of prams full of dirty washing tied on with pieces of old rope. Mums wearing headscarves made up as turbans, with floral aprons pulled over their heads and

tied at the back would gather at the foot of the stairs on the morning of the wash. Some would be smoking cigarettes, dangling from the corner of their mouths and if the weather was cold, top coats straight off the bed would be donned and buttoned up the front. Thick lisle stockings rolled down to their ankles would highlight their red patchwork rash at the back of their legs known as tartan legs which was a result of standing too close, too long with their backs to the fire and their skirts hitched up for warmth. Old flat bockles were worn on their feet to ensure comfort when walking to and from the wash house and for carrying out the required manoeuvres within.

Having reached the pavement at the bottom of the stairs all required items had to be checked; large tin bath which doubled up as the house bath, pile of dirty washing, ensuring nothing had fallen off when the pram was bumped down the stairs. A large bar of yellow sunlight soap was required with a packet of Persil, Rinso or Oxidol soap powder, a scrubbing board and a wash stick for poking, prodding and stirring the washing around the boiling swirling water. Every speck of dirt or fluff from trouser turn-ups and pockets of grimy overalls had to be ejected and stains removed.

A large purse full of change for entry to the wash house and to buy a cup of tea was pushed into the coat pocket. A digestive biscuit and a chocolate one for old Mrs Donnahugh would ensure that an all-important blether incorporating the latest gossip would break out during the morning break.

When all was in order the convoy of women, two abreast, would set off up Grove Street en route to the wash house or steamie; past the Palais and first right at Tolcross School. As they chattered looking left, right, front and behind, they merely held on to the handles and let the prams take themselves forward to their destination. With six or seven women on a mission, no one stood in their way.

The weekly wash was much more than just a cleansing exercise; it was a prime example of community spirit. When someone wasn't well, their dirty washing would be split up between everyone else, washed, hung out to dry and ironed before being returned to them at home

They laughed and joked about men and discussed the reason for any quickly arranged marriages that had taken place. They listened to the latest sad news, cried and wiped the tears from their eyes; consoling one another as problems and difficulties were poured out.

After tea, a whole host of activities followed, including rubbing the clothes up and down on the scrubbing boards, rinsing, squeezing the washing through the large mangles and helping each other to fold the sheets and large items before stacking them back on to the prams which had been left sitting in the designated pram area. Tie and secure the clean clothes for the homeward journey, check no- one left behind in the toilet, everyone present, wagons ready to roll, 'yo oh!!' Homeward bound; they would laugh and laugh again. For some, it was the highlight of the week. Once home, washing would be hung up to air and dry on the pulley in the kitchen.

Small washings were done in the kitchen sink at home and a small scrubbing brush was always to hand for ensuring shirt collars were kept spotless. Hot water was boiled in the large black kettle on the fire and clothes were rinsed under the cold water tap before being put through the wringer which was lifted from the glory hole and on to the sink.

Each family had allocated days for the use of the drying lines in the back greens. Damp washing which could be very heavy, was carried by mums down the stairs to the greens and sometimes two or three journeys were necessary; not to mention carrying it back upstairs again when the drying was complete. On days when lines were full, the community spirit would kick in again and sharing was the norm.

Long poles ensured that the washing lines attached to metal poles or hooks on walls were pushed upwards to prevent the sheets, nappies, towels, hankies and a host of other household clothing from trailing on the ground and to allow the air to circulate around and underneath; assisting in the drying process. Women took a real pride in the whiteness of their clothes and generally preferred not to

hang out their underwear which may in some cases have taken up large areas of the line. Smalls as they were ironically called were rather personal and were usually hung up on the kitchen pulley or even on a string stretching underneath the mantelpiece at the fire.
Washing and drying was followed by ironing. Two metal irons were placed alternately on the coal fire and before use were tested to ensure that they were hot enough by spitting on the face; when hot enough, the spit would run down the length of the face.
Such was technology of the day.

Chapter 21 - Our Street

Various rag and bone men would arrive on the street to exchange goldfish or balloons for old clothes or just rags. One had a small pony and cart, another a large wheelbarrow and all had their individual ways of encouraging folks to bring out their unwanted rags; such as blowing on a trumpet, ringing a Bell, tooting a horn or just shouting up the stairs.

Hannah was different. Hannah would carry her huge bundle of rags wrapped up in a large coloured bed cover which was tied in the middle and left at the bottom of the entrance to each stair prior to her making her way around the doors collecting. I don't think she worried about someone pinching her bundle.

She was small, slightly bent and frail looking but wiry and able to sling her huge sack on to her back as she did her rounds moving from stair to stair. She had fair frizzled hair which had gone grey and was tied at the back in a bun. Her face was wrinkled with the contours of life and her hands were strong with long fingers. The tired tweed shawl lying on slim shoulders was held at the front by a large kilt pin whilst a long black skirt with large patch pockets trailed around her heeled boots laced up the front. She was always very polite and quick to thank anyone who had rags to give her. Folks often slipped in decent jumpers or woollens for her personal use.

Mum and dad always asked her in for a cup of tea, a biscuit, a chat, and a sit down for a wee rest. Gradually her legs were taking longer to climb the stairs and she had to stop for a breather on each landing especially in the cold winter months but she always managed to reach the families who like ourselves lived on the top flats.

One day she quietly passed away. A note was found in her pocket nominating my dad as the executor of her will. She left two hundred pounds in her will with a letter of thanks to mum and dad for their kindness. Dad ensured that she had a decent and proper burial.

Grove Street sloped uphill from Morrison Street to the sawmill where at mid-day the hooter would sound, work stopped and providing that it was dry, the workers would pour outside, sit in a long line with their backs to the wall; covered from head to toe in sawdust, eat their pieces and drink their tea from tin mugs or lemonade straight from the bottle. Often they would give us hovering children the empty bottles to return to the sweetie shop to be redeemed for three pence a bottle.

Next to the sawmill was the railway bridge with peepholes for children to watch the trains passing underneath with clouds of curling smoke coming out of their funnels as they crept into or out of the Waverly Station. Parents would often lift small children up to see the drivers who would pull the cord and blow the whistle as they rolled by.

Onwards past the bridge and ghostly white figures could be seen in the early mornings flitting to and fro from the bakery to the waiting vans for the early morning deliveries to shops around the town. Men and women wore long white aprons covered in flour and small white caps which sat on their heads at jaunty angles to support the boards of freshly baked bread, rolls and varieties of cakes and biscuits being carried out to the vans. The aroma of fresh baking wafted up and down the street and throughout the day, folk turning into Grove Street could be seen closing their eyes, looking upwards, twitching their nostrils, inhaling deeply and smiling.

Further up the street on the left were the stables; a small world of magic for children. Horses were continually coming and going and when Roy Rogers the world famous singing cowboy brought his equally famous horse Trigger to Edinburgh, there waiting for him was the best horse hotel in the world; our stables. Ally my brother and I went up to see Trigger and the groom took us into his stall where we were allowed to pat him. What a magnificent palomino stallion he was with his long flowing white mane and tail that ran through my fingers like a rippling stream.

He was so friendly towards us and kept nudging his nose on to the palms of our hands. The groom said that he was sorry but he couldn't allow us to take him home but he took two long blond hairs from his mane and placed them into a matchbox for us to keep which we did for years to come.

Carrying their flasks and pieces in their ex- army haversacks, men and women went up the street in time for them to clock-in before the hooters went off in the mornings at the sweetie factory, rubber mill and the brewery. Most wore brown coloured or dark overalls and while the women wore turbans made up from headscarves, men kept their heads warm and dry with their bunnets which were also used at home to cool their tea by wafting their caps back and forward over the tea which had been poured into a saucer. Some drunk out of the saucer but that wasn't encouraged in our house.

Many said that they preferred to wear ex- army boots which had been good enough for our lads to chase Gerry across Europe but some preferred clogs.

Chapter 22 - Molly

Brylcream kept the wave at the front of my hair in place until that is, I got my first crew cut at Tony's and although I hadn't lost any curls my mother nearly had kittens and threatened to take me back to the barbers. I'm not sure what Tony could have done as his hair restorer didn't have a great reputation. I certainly didn't need my brylcream any longer.
'You wait till yer dad sees that,' she said. I met dad at the foot of the stairs coming home from work that evening.
'That's some haircut you've got son.' he said. 'It will keep the hair out of your eyes and maybe you'll see better to head that football on your next game. Ye'r mum will be pleased with that,' were the last words on the matter as he went up the stairs. When I was called up for bed later that evening, Mum glowered at me.
The horses pulling carts and drays, lorries, vans, taxies, ordinary folk shopping and carrying out their daily chores mixed with the sounds of babies in prams, children going to school, playing happily after school, created our world of neighbourliness, caring, security, fun, enjoyment of life and just a plain good to be alive life. The smell of fresh hay from the stables at the top of the street, the black curling smoke from the trains rumbling under the bridge were enriched by the fresh aroma of hops from the near- by brewery and the mouth-watering smell of toffee curling up one's nostrils from the sweetie factory, not to forget the aroma of bread fresh out of the ovens circulating from the bakery. The sounds of the morning hooters calling the workers up the hill to the sawmill and rubber mill added to the cacophony of street music creating the atmosphere of our street.
Rugby and football fans en route to Murrayfield and Tynecastle added to the hustle and bustle of the street

which was also a highway to the Palais de Danse at Fountainbridge. Although rock and roll, teddy boys and girls in pony tails had not yet arrived, they were well on their way. It was where we lived and it was our street.
Into this bubbling cauldron stepped Molly with her shaggy grey Shetland Pony, Bobby, pulling a small barrel organ on large wheels. She was elderly in years and stood not much higher than Bobby. Her wrinkled weather beaten face enhanced her large smile as she peeked beneath her headscarf talking continuously to herself, Bobby and the organ. Her gloves were fingerless and she wore a short brown oatmeal coat with patches at the elbows, long woolly ankle socks of different colours and short welly boots. As molly cawed the handle, a myriad of well known tunes rolled off the organ to the delight of us children who would very quickly gather around her to speak to bobby and put some change into her tin box which read thank-you on the front. It was a moment in time that I have always remembered.
At the end of a performance to a large round of applause, Molly would clap Bobby heartily on his shoulders and rub his ear to let him know that he was the star. He would drink from his pail, eat his hay from his wee nose bag and enjoy a carrot or an apple as his reins and the shafts of the organ were checked before moving on.
'What key was the music in?' I remember Lydia Monart asking on one occasion: a smart wee girl who went to piano lessons.
Molly ignored her, thanked everyone for listening and as we clapped and cheered, she gave as always a huge smile which stretched the width of her wrinkled face, blew us all a kiss and waved as she led Bobby down the street but this time she stopped, turned, 'it's the key in to my heart,' she shouted as she waved again and disappeared around the corner towards Haymarket.
One day when I arrived home from school my mother told me that she was taking me to meet the Choirmaster at Saint Mary's Cathedral where I was to be auditioned for entry to the famous school and choir, situated nearby in Palmerston Place.

'Eh?' I asked in disbelief.
'You heard me,' she said.
'Mum, I can't sing.'
'Yes you can.'
'No, I can't and I don't want to change schools. I want to stay with my pals'.
'Yes you can sing. I've heard you.'
'When?'
'Never mind when.' she said.
'Mum, I can't sing.'
'Yes you will.'
We entered the cathedral with its three spires and walked down the long aisle to where some high pitched organ music was being played by a man sitting on a large stool swaying from side to side with his head wobbling around. The sound stopped. 'Ah! Mrs Gee,' he said looking in our direction as his fingers of the right hand ran down the length of the keys from left to right ending the music in grand fashion as if he was bringing an international concert to an end. He stood up and I fully expected him to make a low sweeping bow to my mother.
'I'm Mr Rupert Guscote Pendlington Sharpe and this must be young Howard. I'm delighted to meet you young man. I knew your father when he sang in the choir at Old Saint Pauls. I believe that you go to the Sunday school next door.'
'Yes sir,' I said in my best sheepish little voice.
'Good, good; well let's see how well you can sing. Now just relax, bend your right thumb and place it between your bottom and top teeth. Let the sound come from deep inside your body and up out through your vocal chords. Try to keep in time and in tune with the scale that I will be playing.'
I scowled at my mother who smiled sweetly back at me.
'Now Mrs Gee, if you wouldn't mind standing back and give young Howard the space for the forthcoming sound to reverberate around the apse, I would be grateful; thank you.'
I just wanted to dive under the nearest row of pews.
The keys of the organ were depressed in rapid succession

and after an introductory chord, I received the nod to begin. Nothing came out of my mouth. I took a deep breath; nothing!
‘Let’s try again Howard, shall we?’ I peered around to see if anyone was watching. The nod came and a squeaky sound erupted and turned into a girly squeal as my teeth bit into my thumb.
‘Mrs Gee, I wonder if I could have a word with you in private,’ he said as he drew my mother aside into the shadow of a large nearby pillar. When he returned, he looked me in the eye; ‘well Howard thank- you for coming along and I do hope that you have enjoyed the experience. Your mother will explain all to you. It has been lovely to meet you.’
I had failed. Maybe I was overawed by the cathedral; maybe the minister showing some girls in red blazers around the altar had distracted me or maybe the incense hanging in the air from the funeral that morning had penetrated my lungs.
Maybe I just couldn’t sing.

Chapter 23 - Trespassing

Sometimes instead of steaming through to the west, trains leaving the Waverly Station would roll under our bridge at Grove Street and slip off into the coal depot which stretched out from Morrison Street into Haymarket. As columns of smoke billowed gently out of the funnels, feathers of steam would drift along the engine over the heads of the train drivers and firemen who when they saw us on the bridge would blow the whistle and wave. Trains were often left temporarily in the coal depot until they were stocked up with coal, inspected for repairs or cleaned ready for their next journey.

One Saturday morning six of us sat in the gang hut planning the day's mission.

'There's a long train with carriages sitting in the depot,' said Euan one of the twins.

'There's bound to be one door unlocked,' his twin brother Matt replied. Their kitchen window overlooked the depot which was separated from their back green by a mere six foot wall.

'Right,' I said. 'That's it; decision made. We head for the train.'

'Where are you heading for,' called Marion Taylor as she stuck her head around the door without even giving the secret knock?

'We're heading for the border,' said Hughie sarcastically.

'Lydia and I want to come.'

'Oh, no,' I said. 'It's far too dangerous.'

'Well,' piped up Lydia Monart, 'your mother won't let you go.'

'She doesn't know.'

'She will.'

'That's blackmail.'

'Right,' she said

'Alright, alright,' I said. 'We're cutting down through Ewan's backstairs, over the wall at the back and into the coal depot.
'Are we collecting coal?' asked Marion.
'No,' I said, shaking my head and trying to be patient.
'Are we cleaning a train?' asked Lydia.
'No,' I said, 'we're inspecting one.'
'What do ye mean?'
'Oh come on,' said Billy Macleod, 'before it's left and it's no even there.'
We reached the train and sure enough a door near the front was unlocked. Climbing up and entering involved lifting, pulling, heaving and pushing and was a remarkable achievement in teamwork. Everything about the train seemed huge. The size of the engine wheels, the funnel, the buffers, the height of the carriage door from the ground and the long corridors which we ran along opening and closing doors until we reached the buffet car. Biscuits, crisps, fruit gums and some apples were lying on the counter whilst a bottle of spilt milk could be just seen lying on the floor behind. The goodies were immediately shared out as we piled into a comfortable First Class Carriage laughing and joking as discarded newspapers and magazines were thrown off the seats to make way for some pretend weary travellers.
'Hughie come down from that luggage rack before it breaks,' I shouted.
'I need the toilet,' said Lydia. 'Will you chum me Marion?'
'Aye,' said the other Wally dug.
'Ye'r no getting out,' said Euan, standing in front of the sliding door and preventing it from being opened.
'Hurry up and get out of the way,' pleaded Lydia. 'I'm bursting.'
'Let us out big ears,' bawled Marion in a fit of temper. 'She's desperate.' Marion wasn't known to cry much herself but could she bring tears to the eyes of anyone who stood in her way.
'Hope you can find one,' said Euan sliding the door open and sheepishly standing aside.
With the carriage door open, we could still hear the girls

chattering away to each other as they ran along the corridor to the toilet.
'I'll wait outside the door,' Marion shouted
'Phew!! What a smell,' said Lydia as she pushed the door open.
'Ye'r desperate aren't ye; just get in and get out quick.'
'Right oh Marion, don't get shirky. I'll only be a second.'
We, the boys were sat in the carriage, feet up, stretched out, tucking into the feast and laughing at the comments of the girls when we heard the voice.
'Have you lot got tickets for this train?' came the question from the face beneath the dark blue peaked cap as scrawny hands produced a pair of clippers from the pocket of a long black coat. 'I'm the Ticket Inspector and I want to see your tickets.'
We stopped jumping around and turned towards the tall unshaven, lean looking man who filled the doorway.
'Where's the train going?' asked Ranald.
'If you had tickets you would know,' was the verbally aggressive reply. 'This is the overnight London train and as you lot haven't got tickets, you'll have to get off now or I'll call the police; right now, scram. Get out of this compartment and get off the train or the police with their Alsatian dogs will take the lot of you away in their Black Maria to Saughton Prison.'
'Have you ever been there?' enquired Ranald scowling.
The Inspector had now reached boiling point and was pounding on the glass of the open compartment door with his clenched fists. His face was beetroot red, blue veins were bulging out of his neck and from his mouth a dribble was running down the side of his chin. We froze; were stunned and stood stark still, staring at him.
'I think he's having a fit,' said Ewan.
'The police are here,' shouted Billy, looking out of the window; pointing back towards the guards van.
'What? Where?' said the Inspector pushing Billy aside to see out of the window for himself.
He cursed as he turned, bolted out the door and ran down the corridor towards the front of the train and the engine.
'We'll need to run for it boys,' I shouted.

‘Lydia is stuck in the toilet,’ interrupted Marion who had suddenly appeared. ‘The door’s stuck.’
‘What?’ I shouted. ‘For goodness sake, the police are here.’
‘I’ll try and barge it open with my shoulder,’ said Matt. ‘My mum gave me porridge this morning.’
‘Well done,’ said Ranald; ‘He thinks he’s Popeye,’ I heard him whisper to Hughie.
‘Trust her,’ said Billy as we took off down the corridor following the route of the Ticket Inspector who had opened a carriage door and jumped down to the ground; almost into the arms of a policeman. Dodging the arms of the law, he leapt on to his feet and started to climb upwards on to a huge stack of coal at the rear of the engine where he stood swaying from side to side, wondering what his next move should be. His arms were outstretched as he stepped from one piece of coal to another when suddenly he threw his hands in the air as his knees buckled and he fell forward into the engine where the driver and fireman normally stood. His leg hit the open door of the boiler and he slid down off the engine with his head hitting every step until he reached the ground where he lay quite still.
As I climbed out of the carriage and fell to the ground, the rest of the gang almost landed on top of me. I felt a strong hand grab my collar and yanked me up on to my feet where I faced two uniformed policeman. Three other policemen were running up from the guards van and one was kneeling beside the Ticket Inspector who was lying unconscious
We were immediately informed that we were trespassing on British Railway Property; a serious matter indeed and that our parents would have to be informed.
‘We didn’t know that the train was going to London and that we needed tickets to come on board sir,’ I explained. ‘Is the ticket inspector alright?’
‘His leg is broken and he has a nasty bruise on his forehead,’ said the kneeling policeman looking up at us.
‘He wasn’t a real Ticket Inspector son said the elder of the two policeman. This train was travelling from Inverness to London last night when the toilet system blocked and

stopped flushing. All on board were transferred to another train whilst this one was shunted in here to have the toilets unblocked. This man must have found the ticket inspector's clothing in the guards van.'

'Are you children all okay?'

'Yes sir, I think so,' I replied cautiously

'Are there any more of you in there?' asked the taller of the two policeman and before I could answer, Lydia appeared in the doorway with Marion leaning over her shoulder desperate to find out what was going on.

'Aye there's three more sir,' I said including Matt in my calculations.

'Have you caused any damage in there?'

'No sir,' we all shouted together.

'We didn't push that man out of the train either,' confirmed Billy.

'Did any of you see him fall from the engine?'

'Aye, we all did sir.'

'Did he have a heart attack?' asked Lydia, 'or did he just slip off the coal and fall to the ground?'

'Will we be arrested?' I asked, not bothering to wait for Lydia's question to be answered.

'No son, you won't be arrested. We have an ambulance on its way to take him to the infirmary. I hope that none of you were in those toilets or you'll be in the ambulance too. They must be full of germs and smelling awful.

Marion, with a horrified expression on her face looked at Lydia who shrugged her shoulders, screwed up her face and mumbled something about not being able to wait.

'The plumber has just arrived with the cleaners,' said the policeman, 'and if you've caused no damage you'll probably only go to gaol for twenty years, the standard punishment for trespassing.' He took our names and addresses but seeing the worried look on our faces, he winked, smiled, told us to keep out of the depot in future and to get off home now, before the sentence became forty years. 'I'll put a good word in to the judge for you.'

'Thank you sir,' Lydia said quietly.

'Why have you got your knickers in your hand?' Hughie asked Lydia in his usual observant and forthright way.

‘They’re wet and mind your own business.’
‘What else have you got there Marion?’ Hughie persisted.
‘It’s Toby, Mrs Smith’s cat. We found him curled up and sound asleep behind the buffet counter where he had almost finished a full bottle of milk that had been knocked over. He must have jumped aboard through an open window last night.
‘Are you sure it belongs to Mrs Smith?’ asked the policeman
‘Oh aye sir, that’s Toby,’ we all shouted. ‘We’ll see that he gets home safely,’ which we did.
The following week adults were talking of an article in the Edinburgh Evening News about an escaped prisoner from Saughton Gaol who had impersonated a Ticket Inspector and when chased by some local children had jumped from a train, into the arms of the police injured himself and died on the way to hospital.
Our parents were informed about us trespassing but never really got the full story.

Photographs

Howard and Dorothy Gee
(Dad and Mum)

Howard	Dorothy
27 Jan 1907	1 May 1910
|	|
22 May 1985	21 May 1974

Big Howard and Wee Howard

Self and wee brother Ally

Self and pals
Setting off to Gullane on a cycle run

Milk carts and horses – St Cuthberts Dairy
(Courtesy of 'The Scotsman')

Self, Bobby Douglas, Ally, Eleanor, Mum, and Auntie Marjory at Lawhead Weekend Scout Camp

Dad (far right) in the navy during World War 2

At Portobello
Back: Mary, Eleanor, Dad
Middle: Self, Isobel
Front: Ally, Christine

At The Inch
Ally, Eleanor, and self

Carmine - 11 years

The Palais
(Courtesy of 'The Scotsman')

Carmine at Princes Street Gardens

Chapter 24 - At School

At an early age girls weren't noticed and didn't take part in the cubs, football, rugby, bools, cricket nor British Bulldog but at school when performing Scottish Country Dancing, they came into their own.
Once the dance had been announced they would dash across the gym floor to select their partners. Maggie Scott had a crush on me and there was nothing I could do about it. She looked alright, was clever and I had drawn her for postman's knock at a couple of parties. I think that the draw was rigged but maybe I didn't want to deter her. We were both nine going on ten and she was one week older than me.
The teacher had explained that it was etiquette for boys to ask the girls to dance and that they should go and politely ask the ladies if they would like to dance. Crossing that floor was a nightmare for us manly boys.
One cold winter's day when the snow lay thick on the playground, the girls were in a large huddled group talking about girlie things, laughing and just being happy when the boys attacked from all directions with snowballs. We pelted them until they were screaming and cuddling into each other which made them perfect targets for stuffing snow inside their scarves and down their necks which all ended up in a sobbing, crying debacle involving the teachers and the Headmistress.
Once again I was identified as the ringleader in spite of my plea of innocence. The boys were lined up and given a severe talking to by Miss Simond the Headmistress. 'Someone could have been hurt and I am very displeased at that,' she said and as we were dismissed from her office she looked at me and said, 'for goodness sake Howard Gee will you behave yourself?'
'Yes Miss,' I replied, rather ashamed

Shaking her head as she turned to enter her office, I thought she had a hint of a smile on her face and I felt better.
That afternoon we had Scottish Country Dancing and the first dance was the Gay Gordons. I plucked up my courage, crossed the floor, bowed with my right hand below my chest and my left hand behind my back and politely said to Maggie, 'may I have this dance please?'
She looked at me, stood up, scowled and said, 'Get lost creep.' She brushed past me and strode over the floor to take Callum Smith's hand. He blushed, looked at me and grinned nervously as he led her on to the floor. Spoils of war I thought to myself. I was devastated and humiliated as I crawled back across the floor to sit on an empty bench. That was my first lesson in girlie mood swings.
One day I was chosen to read out a poem to the whole class and I was so pleased;
'A Skelf' (Splinter)
'Ye've hurt yer finger poor wee man, yer pinkie, dearie me
Noo jist ye hud it there till I hae a look and see, my, so ye have, it's a skelf,' etc.
After giving a prize winning rendition, I was made a school monitor but a large number of responsibilities went with the appointment. I had to help the janitor and fellow monitors to deliver the bottles of milk nestling in their metal crates upstairs and into each classroom before the morning Bell went. The bottles, one third of a pint were given to each pupil before playtime. Another important duty was giving out the pens for the writing lesson, ensuring that new nibs were issued only as required. Inkwells were filled from a large bottle of blue ink where a steady hand was a must and messing about was definitely taboo. It was a monitor's duty to ensure at the end of the day that anything lying on the floor such as slates, crayons, small tobacco tins containing a damp rag which was used to wipe the slates clean, pencils, rubbers, rulers etc. were tucked underneath the desks to allow the cleaners to sweep and mop out after all the children had gone home. Long desks were joined to the seat by a curved metal bar and the seat was long enough to sit two pupils side by side.

A monitor's job was also to guide the smaller children through the cloakroom safely but quickly.
When the school bell rang, all pupils lined up in pairs outside in the playground; infants leading and primary seven bringing up the rear. When the duty teacher gave the order to march forward, they did exactly that and entered the school through the large green front door. Infants went into the cloakroom on the ground floor whilst everyone else turned left up the stairs to the tune of The 51st. Highland Division played by Miss Murray on the piano which was situated on the first landing. In through the lower cloakroom, the younger children marched and up some internal stairs to the upper cloakroom where coats, hats, gloves and scarves were hung up on the waiting pegs. The flow of moving, chattering children carrying schoolbags continued out on to the first landing as the older children were entering the lower cloakroom.
'No talking and do keep moving children,' the duty teacher, stationed in the middle of the cloakroom would call at the top of her voice as one or more pupils stopped to pick up a fallen item of clothing resulting in tripping and pushing, bumping and shoving which usually ended up with more coats missing the pegs and even children falling on to the floor.
'Head up, shoulders back, listen to the beat of the music; try to keep in step and stop talking,' she would call out above the noise of laughing, fidgeting children who couldn't hear a word that she was saying. As we reached each landing, children peeled off into their respective classrooms.
Every morning prayers were said before the multiplication tables were repeated by the whole class to the teacher.
The routine was changed every Wednesday when all children marched straight into the hall where the Reverend Harris, the local minister from St. Lukes around the corner would be waiting for us to take part in the singing of a hymn and communal prayers; his favourite prayer was;
'Dear Lord help us each day
To love you more dearly
Follow you more nearly

And understand you more clearly.'
At the morning service, Miss Simond would make any relevant announcements to the whole school.
The hall was used for displaying crafts, wet weather programmes, showing films, any emergencies, gyms, indoor games and races, Nativity Plays, concerts and anything else in between.
Harvest Thanks Giving was special. The Fruits of the trees and the fields were brought to the school by pupils; displayed for all to see and to be blessed by the minister. The large folding tables were always decorative and carefully laid out by the teachers with varieties of flowers, fruit, biscuits, cakes and assortments of food whilst baskets of potatoes, vegetables and tins of soup rested on the floor around the tables. Afterwards everything was given to the local children's home.
'We plough the fields and scatter the good seed on the land,' was the first line of the standard hymn for the occasion. Prayers followed, especially for children who had no parents, were sick, suffered from the many diseases in our world or who lived in Africa and were less fortunate than ourselves.
One year as the service came to a close, we had to leave the hall in class order with the infants leading. As my class passed the display table, someone at the back nudged Donald Campbell who fell into Wally Broon who stumbled, grabbed hold of Rory MacDougal who clung on to me and we all fell under the table which collapsed on top of us; almost buried us alive in cabbages, leeks and tomatoes.
Later that morning as the four of us stood in front of Miss Simond, she expressed her views on the matter. 'I was so embarrassed in front of Reverend Harris,' she said but fortunately he understood that accidents do happen. 'My concern is that I'm not sure that it was an accident but as there is an element of uncertainty, the matter will end here. I am pleased that no one was hurt but believe me,' she said leaning forward to see the whites of our eyes, 'such an accident will not happen next year.'
Cubs, scouts and Braidburn Athletic Club met in and used the school hall for activities and indoor training respectively

in the evenings not to mention whist nights and beetle drives. Mr Mitchell was not only the janitor and scoutmaster but the Coaching Director of the athletic club and had control as to the use of the school facilities.
Another of the monitor's duties was to help the janitor with the school meals when they arrived each morning in a large white van. The large silver coloured sealed metal containers were lifted off the vehicle by the driver and slid along the path from hand to hand by the monitors who had formed a line up to the main door of the school. Mr Mitchell then transferred them by an old porter's barrow into the dining hall to await arrival of the dinner ladies. The empty containers from the previous day were slid back down the line to the van for the return journey to the company that supplied the cooked meals for Edinburgh Education Department.
On bitter cold mornings when Jack Frost was nipping at our fingers and a touch of ice lay on the ground, the empty containers flew down the path at a great speed towards the last monitor standing at the van.
It was on one such morning that Bobby Douglas hurled a container in my direction and George Macdonald shouted on me to duck as a bouncing rubber ball from the playground flew over my head. I took my eye off the container which was hurtling down the path like a snowball gathering speed on a mountainside and it hit my shin and gauged out a piece of my leg. I look at it to-day and still remember that gaggle of girls who had been playing with the ball, running over to me crying 'oh sorry, so sorry, Howard.' Everyone fussed over me which made me feel good and brave. Not a tear that is, until Miss Carruthers made her way through the crowd with a pad soaked in dettol and dabbed it straight on to raw flesh. No warning. No anaesthetic, nothing. I was just about to pass out when I saw Ellen Robertson looking at me closing her eyes and tutting at my please give me sympathy look. Through sheer strength of character, I managed not to whimper.
School dinners were nearly always soup on Mondays accompanied by a roll and a piece of cheese, followed by cake and custard although the midweek menu varied from

meat and fish accompanied by shredded carrots, salad, potatoes, turnip or cabbage. Mince and tatties were popular whilst cake and custard every day was boring and awful. Frog's spawn (sago) was sometimes given as a welcome change in the pudding.

We moaned and groaned about school dinners but more importantly, we were always hungry and sometimes we did get offered seconds.

Chapter 25 - The Thief

I was a member of the Junior Section of the Braidburn Athletic Club that met weekly in the premises of the school dining room.

The dinner hall benches were used for laying our clothes on when we changed into running gear or tracksuits to go out for a training run. When the senior athletes returned from their training runs around the Harrison and Roseburn Parks, the long dinner tables were ideal for flopping onto and having their aching muscles massaged by the coach and trainers. The aroma of liniment hung in the air and on Beetle Drive and Whist nights, noses were continually sniffing and twitching. Windows were left open for the smell to be wafted out by the waving of towels at the end of the night in readiness for school dinners the following day.

I well remember Rab Thomson's granny commenting one Friday night at the whist that if she could have her chist rubbed by the coach with some of that stuff, her whist would improve no end.

Although I would be helping with other cubs to give out the tea and biscuits and collect the cups and saucers afterwards, I was sometimes asked to stand in as a partner if a table was short of a player at the whist. My auntie Annie had taught me to play and I think that I was quite a good player although I often got scowled at if I played the wrong card and lost the hand.

On certain days each year, the Bell would sound for fire drill to commence. The whole school immediately stopped what they were doing, stood up at their desks and were ushered out of the classrooms by their teachers and downstairs in an orderly and speedy manner into the playground: no chatter, no nonsense. We lined up outside in our classes and were told to look up at the pretend burning building which was engulfed by pretend flames. A debateable intelligent discussion would take place amongst the pupils as to whether or not they were glad that the school was not burning down; after all they had left their school bags inside with their sweets and play pieces inside them. It was always disappointing that the fire engines didn't come screaming down Orwell Place.

We often wondered what all the fuss was about. Secretly we enjoyed school and were quite pleased that it hadn't burned down as what would we do if there was no school the following day? 'Oops, it was Saturday; aw great!'

One late Sunday afternoon, four of us were cycling home from Corstorphine Woods via the Belford Bridge and beyond to Palmerston Place. As we approached the cathedral, a tall long haired, bearded man in shirt sleeves and dark trousers ran past us in the opposite direction clasping what looked like a handbag.

A short distance further on, lying on the pavement was an old lady shouting for help. She was shaking and sobbing; obviously in a state of shock.

'He knocked me down and stole my handbag,' she said in between tears rolling down her cheeks and into the corner of her mouth. 'Will you help me please?'

'We will,' we all shouted, 'we are boy scouts.'

As I was a seconder in the scouts, I assumed organisational responsibility and told Wally Broon to cycle to the nearby police station at Torphican Place; 'explain the situation and tell them that an ambulance might be needed although there were no obvious injuries to be seen. Tell them that she is lying on the ground and may have banged her head. Donald you stay with the lady, talk to her and try to comfort her but don't tell her any of your daft jokes. Bobby, grab your bike and we'll see if we can find that thief.' I hadn't even thought about how we were going to apprehend him if we did find him. We never saw him again but found the empty handbag which the lady, a Mrs Oliver confirmed to the police as hers.

Between us we were able to give the police who called to take a statement from us at school the next day, a good description of the man. Miss. Simond said that we had been very brave and that my training in the boy scouts had been a major factor in taking control of a very worrying situation, helping a citizen in distress and the police in carrying out their duties in maintaining law and order on our streets. She was sure that one day I would be promoted to a patrol leader in the scouts and that she would inform Mr Mitchell the janitor who happened to be the scoutmaster. With head held high, I felt obliged to remind her that we were all in the scouts and that it had been a team effort. I'm sure in her mind she was thinking what a nice boy, young Howard Gee is. 'Could this be the same boy who has frequented my office on so many occasions for the wrong reasons?' she was probably asking herself.

A few days later, the four of us were called back to Miss. Simond's office to be informed that a man had been arrested and charged with the crime. A letter of thanks had arrived and was read out to us by Miss Simond. Mrs Oliver had recovered from her ordeal and wished to thank us for helping her in her hour of need. 'You have been a credit to your school, the scouts and a shining example to all young children,' she had written. 'Thank you all so much, you have made an old lady very happy to know that people and in this case children do care and think about helping older folks in their hours of need.'

For the rest of the day, we were real heroes at the school although nobody asked us for our autographs.

Chapter 26 - Raw Sewage

It was a quiet sunny weekend when with our towels tucked under our arms; no swimming costumes needed, a crowd of us from the street decided to go for a swim in our secret pool in an area known to us as The Tips on the Water of Leith.

Reaching the Belford Bridge, we squeezed through some broken iron railings, past the 'Danger: No Trespassing' sign, down the slope avoiding the 'No Entry' sign and through some bushes to the water's edge. To reach the part of the river which had been dammed by boulders taken from the river bed by ourselves over the summer months, we had to follow a left hand bend in the river until it disappeared under some overhanging willow trees. The rippling water fed the deep pool created by the dam but continued to flow gently over and between the boulders and meander downstream. A rope which we had tied to a tree leaning out over the pool was ideal for a Tarzan Swing and with a long run off the bank and knees up; we could reach the middle of the pool before letting go; resulting in a mighty splash. Two or three clinging to the rope at the same time was great fun but daringly tricky as the branch could have snapped at any time. Our theory however was that we would land in the water with an even bigger splash causing us to have an even bigger laugh and we just didn't worry about it.

Prior to reaching our secret spot, we had to negotiate a very large round black pipe which traversed an open sewer of bubbling effluent yellow and green sewage. At one time in the distant past there had been a wooden cover over the pit but it had disappeared one year around bonfire night, on the fifth of November. None of us were sure how deep the pit was as it had never crossed our minds to think about it.

It was agreed that I would cross first and hold out a long

branch in case someone hesitated and needed to grab it to steady themselves. I was followed by Wally Broon and Billy Macleod. Ranald decided that he could walk it backwards and Ronnie Nesbit despite my shouting at him not to, announced that he could do it with his eyes shut, well nearly shut. Ewan and Matt Baxter, the twins sat astride the pipe and edged along it. Last but one to cross was 'Titch' Cameron who hadn't done it before and was obviously very nervous. His mother had rubbed his chest that morning with menthol smelling vic to help him fight off a niggling cough and an oncoming cold.

'Ye'r alright,' shouted Mac, 'I'm right behind you.'

It was just about the half-way point when Mac decided to do his balancing act. He stopped and shouted for everyone to look at him as he lifted his right knee up, wavering on his left leg with outstretched arms. I held my breath and shut my eyes. Titch turned his head to see what was happening behind him and toppled straight into the sewage. Mac tried to catch him but followed him in. We stood open mouthed and dumbstruck as they disappeared below the surface. Before we could react, two heads attached to two bodies bobbed up resembling gruesome monsters of the deep. Mac stood up and was waist deep whilst Titch was in the raw sewage up to his chin.

We burst out laughing but cried tears of relief and joy that they had appeared and were alive. They were spluttering, coughing and spitting out yellow, green and dark purple gunge which was running off their hair, over their eyelids, into their mouths, on to their chins and downwards on to their chests. The smell was foul and reminiscent of a concoction of human waste, vomit and rotten vegetables with other unknown ingredients thrown in which of course was exactly what was bubbling and gurgling in there. A witch's brew would have smelt like roses and honeysuckle compared to the smell emanating from that pit.

Pulling them out with every effort to ensure that we didn't slip and join them was strenuous but we hauled them out and they flopped on to the bank. Everyone had raw sewage splattered on their clothes and I suggested that the best solution for all of us, was to run along to the pool, a

few hundred yards away and jump straight in. 'We needn't bother to take our clothes off,' I said.
As we had to walk home, we dispensed with the idea of having a bonfire and throwing our clothes on to the flames but rather to hang them up on a branch of a tree and attempt to let dry.
We ran and jumped off the bank into the pool, swam and played in the bare buff, swung on the Tarzan Swing, and tumbled around in a world of freedom. We laughed and joked with each other all the way home and couldn't stop talking about the rescue but I remember saying my prayers of thanks that night.
A few days later Mac and Hamish took ill. Mac recovered quickly but Titch developed scarlet fever and after a spell in hospital only just survived.
It was a long time before we went to The Tips again but we did find a different route to our pool which by-passed the sewage pit.

Chapter 27 - Trip To Gullane

When the leaders of the Faith Mission from the hall in Morrison Street came round the stairs of Grove Street asking parents if their children would like to come along on a Sunday evening to join with those gathering to listen to stories about Jesus and sing happy songs, it seemed a good idea especially when we children heard that free sweeties would be given out. There was also the promise of cream cakes, ice cream, games and lots of fun if we went to the annual picnic at Gullane by the seaside.

Some of the gang and even three or four of the girls agreed to try it and we all did. On the first night, we were met at the door, made very welcome and ushered up the stairs to the meeting hall where we sat on long benches facing a wooden platform. Three ladies in Salvation Army look alike bonnets entered, nodded to us and smiled. When two men in dark blue jackets came in we were asked to stand but Mary Scobbie refused and continued to look down, her ankles crossed and her feet swinging under the bench. One of the smiling female leaders changed her smile to a frown but was completely ignored by Mary.

Standing up one of the men stepped forward to a lectern, looked around the room and seemed to fix his gaze on all of us new recruits to the mission. He was stocky, balding, had silver buttons down the front of his tunic and wore lapel badges in his jacket. His rounded face resembled the man on the moon portrayed on the creamola packets but his white shirt and black tie matching his black shoes introduced a touch of officialdom especially with his pug nose holding up his glasses which he peered over towards our bench. We cowered but he smiled warmly and spoke in a very grown up way with a deep voice. 'Welcome, very welcome to you all and thank you for coming.

Have you washed in the blood of the lamb?' he asked.

'What's he saying?' asked Jimmy Macleod in a loud voice.
'Wheesht!' replied Lydia Monart.
'Have you washed in the blood of the lamb?' the question was asked again.
'I washed last night in the sink,' shouted Shuggie Clelland who toppled sideways as Helen Mackay elbowed him in the ribs. The whole hall burst out laughing, at least all of us children did.
'A good answer,' said the man on the platform 'and tonight we are going to tell you about Jesus who suffered, bled and died for us on the cross that we might have our sins forgiven and have everlasting life.'
'We haven'ae sinned,' said Mary Scobbie.
'No we haven'ae,' repeated Lydia.
'I think that we have all sinned at some time or another but Jesus will save and forgive us if we ask him and so there is no need to worry if you will only come to him.' the man said looking around the room and speaking in a very understanding way.
'Hymm!' sighed Mary. 'I wonder where Jesus lives.'
'Sheest!' said Lydia again getting madder by the minute
'I will now ask Miss Jenny and Miss Linda to lead us in our first song of the evening and as there are actions, I think that we should all stand up; if that's all right with you Mary.'
When everyone stood up, Mary followed.
'We will have a quick rehearsal first, to ensure that we can all hear the piano and do try to keep in tune,' chirped Miss Linda. 'When you are ready Miss Amelia, we'll begin.'
Reading the words on a large sheet of paper hanging on a blackboard easel the whole gathering started to sing and the new members although very unsure of themselves at first slowly joined in. Miss Amelia beaming brightly gave it laldy on the piano accompanied by Miss Jenny on her tambourine and we burst into song.
'Deep and wide, deep and wide, there's a fountain flowing deep and wide.'
After the first verse we had mastered the actions and sang with great gusto and it was good fun. We left the hall one hour later chattering and shouting 'cheerio see you next week.'

When the bus left the Mission Hall for the annual picnic to Gullane, it was packed with noisy excited children. Although hanging toilet rolls out of the bus windows was forbidden, coloured streamers were popular and agreed upon by the accompanying adults. Weather was always pre- arranged and the sun was shining down on us as we stepped off the bus. It was one of the benefits of having Jesus on our side.

Instructions were given out about general behaviour, being careful when running around and the use of official toilets only. After the whistle was blown, there was a mad dash down to the water's edge, a jump in and a jump out when the cold water splashed up the knees via the ankles. Buckets and spades were immediately utilised in digging holes and making sand castles. We paddled and the bravest of the brave swam but shivered and wrapped towels tightly around themselves when they came out. Men stripped down to their vests or even their bare chests, tied hankies on their heads to protect them from the sun that we had been praying for, rolled their trouser legs up and ran along the sand kicking footballs and generally aired their varicose veins.

It wasn't long before a couple of jerseys were thrown down to act as goalposts at opposite ends of a stretch of sand and a football game was underway. Nobody worried about teams being equal nor where the boundaries should be; children ran after the ball and that was all that mattered.

Women in bare feet hitched their dresses up and took special care of the little ones as they splashed about in the shallows. Rocks were rolled over and pools peered into for crabs or any other creatures crawling from under clumps of seaweed. Although we had been well warned to stay clear of anything that resembled a jelly fish which could sting and cause a nasty rash, we still dared each other to touch them and we did.

After the organised races, we climbed the dunes and rolled down head over heels in the warm, soft, rippling sand. We laughed all the way down and laughed as we climbed all the way up again but when the whistle blew for food, the charge of The Light Brigade could not have moved faster.

Sandwiches with every possible kind of filling from sandwich spread and corn beef to raspberry and strawberry jam; pies, sausage rolls, crisps, scones, pancakes, cream cakes, jam rolly polly, doughnuts, chocolate biscuits, trifle, fruit, ice cream and jelly. Orange squash and lemonade were the popular drinks.

Rounders, various games such as tig, throwing and catching beach balls, chasey and hide and seek were organised and had children running, shouting, falling over and having fun in the sand; maybe they had found Jesus in their own way.

Half an hour of free time was announced before it was time to go home when children were asked to ensure that they had all items of clothing including shoes before boarding the bus.

Prior to leaving our picnic site, all rubbish was collected, put into sacks and taken home with us for dispensing into the huge bins at the back of the Mission Hall. On the way home, we sang our hearts out knowing all the words and actions from the songs we had learnt at the Mission, Band of Hope, Sunday school, cubs and brownies.

'I'm H A P P Y, I'm H A P P Y
I know I am, I'm sure I am
I'm H A P P Y.'

A big cheer and applause erupted at the end of each song. Silence was then called for to allow the leaders to demonstrate the actions of the next song and then straight into

> 'My cups full of running over
> For the Lord saith me, I'm as happy as can be
> My cup's full of running over.'

Before we got off the bus back at the Mission Hall, we all joined in a big thank-you to all who had organised such a marvellous day for us and gave three very loud cheers for them.

Happy innocent days drifted by with summer.

Chapter 28 - Picnic At Porty

Arriving home from school one day, I ran up the stairs, turned the corner and just before the first landing, I bumped into Isobel who lived next door to us and was charging down the stairs. She was a year older than me although slightly smaller in height and usually wore a clasp or ribbon in her short, fair hair.
'Sorry,' we both said in unison.
'What's your hurry?' she asked.
'Nothing,' I said, 'I'm just going to get changed into my old clothes and then out to play football.'
'Howard, your mum has just told me that we're all going for a picnic to Porty (Portobello) on Sunday.'
'Oh great!' I said.
'But,' she continued, 'it's only if you keep out of trouble and behave yourself. Please try.'
'Right,' I said as she disappeared down the stairs. I turned the key in the lock, opened the front door and burst into the kitchen where mum was just making a cup of tea. 'Great news!' I shouted, 'guess what mum? We are all going on a tram to Porty on Sunday. We can have candy floss, a ride on the shows and the donkeys and if I'm really good maybe even on the Donald Duck Boat.'
'Slow down,' said mum, 'when did you plan all this?'
'Just now, coming up the stairs,' I fabricated.
'Where's the money coming from to pay for it all?' she asked, looking at me in trepidation as to what my answer might be.
'We'll think of something mum, don't worry.' She rolled her eyes and shook her head in that familiar negative manner that I had become accustomed to.
'Dad and I have decided to take Isobel, Mary and their mum along with us for a day out to Portobello. Auntie Kate Grant and your cousin Christine are down from Perth for a

couple of days and will be coming with us. You will be able to come too if you behave yourself.'
'Right, mum. Are Eleanor and Ally coming to?'
'Of course your sister and brother are coming. Do you think that we would leave them behind. I know who might be left at home if he doesn't stop getting into mischief.' I looked down at the linoleum and ignored that unfair and harsh comment.
'Can we sit up front in the family compartment of the tram?'
'Well let's wait and see if we are going first,' said mum looking at me again with that exasperated look. 'Now go and change out of your school uniform.'
I said my prayers on Saturday night and the sun was shining Sunday morning. 'You don't need to go to Sunday school,' said mum.
'Oh! what a shame,' I replied.
'Don't be cheeky, shouted dad,' his lips moving from underneath a thick white lather of shaving soap. 'Just hurry up and get dressed and see if you can help your mother finish making up the rolls for the picnic. Let's get away while the sun is still shining.'
'Right dad, I'll tell Ally and Eleanor to get ready.'
' Ally, You've to hurry up and help mum with the rolls.'
'Why me?' shouted Ally trying to keep his balance whilst pulling on his underpants
'Dad said so. Hurry up, if you don't want to be left behind. Eleanor and I are sitting up front in the tramcar.'
'I'm coming as fast as I can mum,' shouted Ally.
'Take your time, said mum, just make sure that everything goes on properly and the right way round after you've washed and combed your hair. Isobel and Mary have come in to help me; their mum is allowing them to be excused morning mass at the chapel. At last we were ready to go and we made our way to the tram stop, just past the police station at Torphican Place. We were laden with bags full of goodies, buckets and spades, rolled up towels with swimming costumes, rain coats in case the weather changed and everything else that was mandatory for a picnic at the seaside.
The almost empty tram rolled up from Haymarket and mum

and dad stepped back to let us children lead the way upstairs. The conductor stood at the bottom of the stairs and I heard him mumble as we passed him, 'there goes my peaceful Sunday morning run to Portobello.' With his eyes fixed on the large circular mirror at the turn of the stairs, he followed our progression up the stairs and into the aisle. He jingled the change inside his leather shoulder satchel with his right hand, held on to the safety rail with his left and stretched his neck upwards and around the spiral staircase 'Take your time now, there's room for all,' he bellowed

As we dashed along the corridor to the front compartment, Ally dropped his towel; I tripped and almost rolled into the laps of two old ladies who had been enjoying a peaceful Sunday morning and the view of Edinburgh from the upstairs window of the tram.

'Sorry,' I said as I straightened myself up.

'As long as you're alright son,' one said. 'You enjoy your day at the seaside, you're only young once.' They both smiled before turning to gaze out of the window again.

Mary reached the sliding door at the front first but couldn't get it opened. Ally stretched across slid it open and we all slumped into the long half-moon seats.

'Quick shut the door,' shouted Isobel.

'Aye,' said Ally, 'the adults can sit outside.'

We disembarked at Portobello High Street and followed the crowds to the sand and the sea. A mass of people carrying baggage, holding on to small children who were pulling, tugging and shouting for ice cream; all heading for fresh air, warmth, relaxation and fun; oh and a suntan. It must have been a similar picture to that of the Israelites leaving Egypt and heading for the Red Sea and freedom. Everyone was taking deep breaths and filling their lungs with the fresh air carrying nature's goodness on the sea breeze. As we reached the promenade and looked over the waist high barrier down on to the beach, we all as one stopped dead in our tracks. There wasn't any vacant sand to be seen. My jaw dropped. There were bodies everywhere, sitting on deck chairs, sprawling on towels; running, jumping, building sandcastles using their buckets and spades and even burying screaming siblings up to their necks in sand. Men were stretched out sleeping in their vests with trousers rolled up. Braces worn with the belt ensured that their trousers stayed up above the waistline. Hankies were worn on their balding heads to keep off the sun and a knot tied at each corner ensured that they stayed on. Women paddling with small children had tucked their dresses up into their bloomers above the knees.

I looked at dad with big spaniel like eyes. 'Don't worry son.' He said. 'We'll walk along the prom a wee bit. There's a bit of sand, just along a wee bit; waiting for us.'

'There!' screamed Ally pointing to an empty patch of beckoning golden sand.

I never did find out how my dad knew about that bit of sand waiting for us.

'Right,' said dad taking control of the situation. 'Go and stake our claim on that piece of sand.' We ran down the nearest ramp almost treading all over the laid out picnic of a family that looked so well organised that they must have been there all night. I spread my towel out on the sand and the others followed.

Mum's voice arrived over the cacophony of surrounding noise. 'For goodness sake, lift those towels up now. You don't know what's been lying on that sand. Dad will pay for deck chairs.'

Ally and I helped dad carry the three chairs over to mum who was organising our spot. The attendant renting out the chairs didn't mention about requiring a university degree to erect them.

'Why don't the bairns wrap towels around themselves, get changed into their costumes and run down to the sea for a paddle,' suggested Jeanie.

'A good idea,' said dad 'and we'll have a cup of tea, a wee bit of shortbread and some peace. Isobel you and Howard are the eldest and in charge. I'll be able to see you from here and if you have any problems just wave to me. Remember you are only paddling. Eleanor you are the youngest and you are to do as you're told.'

'Yes Dad,' she answered

I was so determined to be first into the water that I put both feet into the one leg of my trunks and as I stumbled, my towel fell down to my ankles.
'Look!' said Eleanor. All heads turned in my direction. I was mortified, grabbed the towel and fell over on to the sand. I was so embarrassed but even worse, Ally was first in.
After the dip in the sea and a brisk rub down, we sat on the sand around the deck chairs and tucked in to the feast that mum and Jeanie had prepared and washed it all down with gallons of lemonade. Dad stood up, stretched his tired limbs and stifled a yawn. 'Must be the sea air,' he said. 'I'm going up to the shops on the esplanade. Would anyone like me to bring back an ice-cream, candy floss or a toffee apple? You all have a choice.'
'Yes, me!' was the loud response. It was agreed that Mary, Christine and Eleanor would accompany dad to remember him who had ordered what, whilst the rest of us children began digging a huge hole to reach Australia. When we realised that we weren't going to get there, we started building a large sandcastle with a surrounding wall and moat which we filled with water by running up and down to the water's edge with our buckets. Unfortunately as quick as we filled the moat, it drained away into the sand. After wakening mum and Jeanie from their slumber in the warm sunshine and whilst waiting on dad and the girls to return with our selected goodies, we decided to bomb the castle and began jumping all over it.
Mum had brought the little Brownie box camera and took photographs as we queued up for a ride on the donkeys of which there were seven. By luck six became free at the same time and the assistants were adept at holding the reins with one hand while helping the children on to the saddle with the other. My donkey had an older girl in charge and she asked me if I'd like a hoist up. 'No thank you,' I said indignantly remembering seeing the film where Geronimo the famous Apache Chief, escaping from the U.S. Cavalry, leapt on to a horse from behind and galloped off, all in one movement. I plucked up courage and went for it. My rear end reached the saddle but didn't stop on it and I went flying over the donkey's back and down on to the

sand beyond.
'Are you alright?' asked the girl, mumbling under her breath 'smart Aleck' and obviously being more worried about the donkey.
Jumping up quickly with a very red rash that I could feel spreading over my cheeks, I said, 'yes, I'm fine.' Mum was concerned but still managed to snap a photograph of me rubbing my behind and brushing the sand out of my hair and ears. Everyone had a good laugh as we trotted up the beach single file with my donkey bringing up the rear. 'It wasn't fair,' I thought to myself.
The Donald Duck boat was a popular treat and as it left its stand on the beach and drove down across the sand and into the sea, it was always surrounded by cheering, waving children, no doubt wishing that they were aboard. As it powered its way out to sea, passengers sat along the sides and enjoyed the waves lapping over their trailing hands.
'Can we go on the boat?' Ally asked.
'Oh yes please,' we all shouted at once.
'Well,' said dad, 'it's two shillings for adults and one shilling and three pence for children. Sorry, it's just far too expensive but you can all have one ride each at the fun fair.'
'Hooray!' the cheer went up. While mum and Jeanie continued to stretch out and relax in the sunshine, dad took us up to the shows. Isobel and I chose the waltzer. Ally and Mary preferred the dodgem cars whilst Eleanor sat with dad and Christine on the carousel. The music throughout the fairground was melodic and intermingled with the cries from the stall assistants. People moving in all directions talking and laughing loudly added to the excitement of the moment. Dad appeared to be so pleased at seeing us children happy that as we passed between the coconut shy and hoopla stall, he decided to give us all a special treat and led us through to the helter skelter. 'Three goes for sixpence,' cried the man in charge smiling as he spotted six new potential customers.
'Right,' said dad, 'collect your mats and off you go. I'll wait at the bottom. Be very careful climbing the stairs and keep your elbows in to your sides.' We closed our eyes and

screamed as we hurtled down and around the corkscrew bends until we shot off the end of the chute on to the rough matting. We couldn't stand up and climb back up the stairs quick enough for another go. This time we all hunched up close, legs spread and arms reaching around the one in front as we came down in train fashion. It was fun, fun, fun.

On the way back to the beach, we stopped to look at a shop with picture postcards on a rotating stand outside the front door. All had humorous poses by very fat ladies in embarrassing positions and saucy comments by gawping men.

Back on the beach, we ran down to the sea where we made sand pies, rolled on the soft sand and shouted, 'Oh no!' When mum announced it was time to go home.

'Five minutes then', said dad.

'Ten minutes,' pleaded Eleanor with her hands clasped and that angelic look on her face. She had a way of persuading dad with that look.

'Okay but no more.' said dad rolling his eyes, knowing at the start of negotiations that he would lose in the end.

'Thanks dad, you are the best dad in the whole world,' said Eleanor blowing dad a kiss. Dad smiled and waved as we all ran down to the waves again.

When the dreaded moment came, everything was packed up and shaken free of sand.

'Leave your sandals off until we are up on the promenade,' said mum who as usual was always thinking ahead. 'You can sit on the wall and brush the sand out from your toes.'

'Right mum.'

On the way back to the tram stop, having checked that all bags and items were accounted for including children, we stopped to buy a poke of chips with salt, vinegar and sauce spread all over the chips. We reached home and climbed the stairs to our top flat; tired weary but still chattering, laughing and feeling very happy.

I knew that, we would always remember that day. We stopped on the landing before turning the keys in their respective locks and said thank-you to mum, dad and Jeanie for that picnic and special fun day at Porty.

Chapter 29 - Christmas Eve.

Dopey our brown and ginger cat slept on his blanket in the glory hole awoke, scratched his ear and washed his face by licking his paw and rubbing it over his nose and eyes. His freedom of the house was through a small window that led into the hall. As he stretched his back and long legs, he knew with cat's intuition that this Saturday night was sing song night in the house and there would be lots of adults screeching at the top of their voices with pushing, pulling, stumbling, irritating children everywhere. There would however be lots of crumbs from iced cakes and delicious titbits falling off the table into his clutches and beneath the safety of the large table cover he would patiently wait and devour them at ease. He often grinned, licked his lips and when his whiskers bristled, we knew that he was thinking of food.

Dad was gifted musically and had taught himself to play the Baby Grand deep reddish, coloured piano which sat in the corner with the lid propped up in the big room. It was a shining light, beckoning to one and all for musical Saturday nights at the Gee's house but this night was special as it was Christmas Eve. It wasn't a case of who was invited but rather how many friends and neighbours with their children could be squeezed in.

It was snowing outside and a warm crackling fire was roaring up the lum inside as we all settled into the warmth of the big room in the house. Throughout the afternoon, we children had sat in a circle, finishing off homemade paper chains and decorations to hang from the ceiling and stretch across the room from wall to wall. The Christmas tree was laden with glittering bobbles, small boxes of pretend presents and dabs of white cotton wool for a snowy wintery effect. We didn't have fairy lights but a star looked down from the top of the tree to remind us all that it was shining

on the stable where the baby Jesus was born. Eleanor's small doll dressed in a white shawl, lying amongst the straw in a little manger with cut out cardboard kings, shepherds, cattle and an ass standing around was the heart of our Christmas Eve.
Women sat on every available surface listening and blethering at the same time as only women have the skill to do. Children were everywhere, playing hide the thimble, riding on the large rocking horse standing beside the back wall and generally getting excited and ready for Christmas morning.
'Right!' said mum, 'let's have a pause for eats.'
'Yeah!!' was the loud response.
Mum poked her head into the kitchen, 'Everyone ben the hoose for something to eat; now please.' she shouted. Returning to the hustle and bustle of the big room, she switched off the light and in the darkness, there was an immediate silence. She switched the light on and after the initial cheer, she had everyone's attention. 'Would all children try to find somewhere to sit down please; cross legged on the floor will do. Hold your plates on your knees and the adults will pass the food along; try and lift it on to your plates without dropping it. The older girls will help the wee ones; won't you girls?'
'Yes, Mrs Gee,' Isobel replied smiling at the opportunity to be helpful and capable of holding responsibility.
Carried out from the kitchen came the sandwiches, hot sausage rolls and pies, buns ,cakes, scones, mince pies and varieties of Christmas homemade baking. Drinks preceded ice cream and jelly whilst paper hats and crackers were in abundance. We children scoffed until we were full and then ate some more.
'Hope you all feel like singing now,' shouted dad as he sat down on the piano stool ready for business, wearing his sleeveless Fair Isle pullover. He ran his fingers up and down the keys with practised dexterity ending in a loud drawn out chord which had the desired effect of creating silence. All eyes turned towards dad at the piano. 'Here we go then,' he said. 'I will now be accompanied by Arthur Sheppey who has travelled all the way from downstairs

carrying his accordion with him not to mention Bertha his good lady wife.' Cheers and handclapping by all. 'Helping us along with his harmonious harmonica,' dad continued, 'from just around the corner is Uncle Tam Reeves. Auntie Jean has agreed to lead us in the singing.'
More cheers and clapping.
'Are you sitting comfortably and are all the children down the front and ready to sing?'
A loud 'yes,' erupted and the question was answered.
'Well,' said dad, 'we're off this time with Rudolph the Red Nose Reindeer.' The piano led the way and the children who needed no encouragement were straight into it; the words reverberated around the room.
Willie, Harry and Johnny Dingwell who lived in a flat on the landing below, were getting on a bit in years, a bit shaky on their legs and didn't get out much but they never failed to climb up to our top landing for the Gee's sing song nights, especially on Christmas Eve. 'It's snowing outside,' cried Harry. 'I think we should sing Jingle Bells. Who knows the words?'
'Me!!' came the immediate, loud response from all the children and as they dashed over to the window, noses were rubbed up against the window panes to see the falling snow. In the light thrown from the street lamps it was truly a winter's wonderland outside although it was just a wee bit early for Santa and his sleigh to be passing by. Listening to the selected key on the piano, Auntie Jean led us straight into, 'Dashing through the snow, on a one horse open sleigh.' The whole room burst into song, jumping up and down to the chorus of
'Jingle Bells, jingle Bells, jingle all the way,'
'What's that tapping noise on the floor?' asked Uncle Bob Lorimer cupping his hand to his ear.
'Oh don't worry,' answered dad, 'that's old Corky, Mr Coughland who lives below us complaining about the noise that our feet are making on the floor. He's tapping on his ceiling with a broom handle. I had invited him up with his sister Isa but it seemed that they were too busy. It is Christmas Eve you know,' he told me.
'Uncle Tam,' said a wee voice escaping from a mouth full

of cake. 'Can we please have some stories with shadows on the wall?' asked Wilma Craig the owner of the voice.
'Oh yes please Uncle Tam,' shouted the unanimous vocal support.
'Okay,' said Uncle Tam flexing his fingers. 'It will give Big Howard a break from the piano. Would all the children please sit round to face the wall. I'll adjust the small lamp if Dorothy, you wouldn't mind switching off the main light and when you are all sitting quietly, I'll begin.'
With his intertwining fingers and thumbs, Tam cast shadows on to the wall which could be recognised easily and we children responded with great gusto and delight.
'It's Pluto, Tom the Cat, a duck and two hens fighting over a piece of bread. It's Popeye.' came a voice from the centre of the group.
'How do you know it's Popeye?' asked Uncle Tam.
'Because he's got a pipe in his mouth and his muscles are huge,' answered Billy Macleod.
'And Olive Oil, his wife comes next,' cried Lydia Monart, a smart wee girl who went to Gillespie School for posh children.
Uncle Tam continued through his routine with infectious laughter and rapturous applause from his audience. 'Now for the finale,' he announced conjuring up a small boy sitting on a moving carpet wearing an Egyptian fez with his arms pointing forwards and upwards.
Lydia again, portraying her extensive knowledge of history, fables and literature came to the fore; 'It's Sinbad the Sailor on his magic carpet flying over the rooftops of Bagdad.'
'Well done Lydia,' cried Uncle Tam 'and thank-you all for watching.'
'A big hand for Uncle Tam,' shouted dad. Children and adults alike applauded, and cheered; with a beaming smile the wizard with the magic hands took his bow.
'Can I go to the toilet please Mrs Gee?' asked Ronnie Nesbit.
'Us too?' asked the twins Ewan and Matt. With their fair curly hair, it was difficult at a glance to tell them apart although one had a slight squint in his left eye but I could never remember which one.

‘Can I go too Mrs Gee?’ asked Mary Scobbie
‘Of course you can,’ answered my mother. ‘You can all go but the boys must go first as they will be quicker. Howard will show you the way and where the key is kept. No nonsense now. Are you listening Howard? Howard do you hear me? There is to be no nonsense now, I mean it. Leave the lobby light on and just pull the front door to.’
‘Yes mum. Why does she always talk to me in front of my pals as if I’m a child?’ I asked myself.
More instructions from mum were on their way. ‘The toilet key is where it’s always kept Howard, hanging on the nail behind the front door. Don’t lose it and boys do remember to lift the toilet seat up before piddling. Isobel can take any of the girls who need to go after the boys return. Howard ensure that the toilet light is left on for the girls and all of you remember to wash your hands at the kitchen sink; there’s a bar of soap and a towel ready for you,’ my mother rambled on without pausing for breath.
The four of us boys squeezed into the toilet and just managed to get the door shut when Ronnie asked why it was only the boys that had to lift the toilet seat and before someone thought of an answer, he asked what the letters H.G. carved on the underside of the wooden seat meant.
‘Well,’ I said, pausing and trying to think of an appropriate answer. ‘Do you remember that penknife that Jimmy Brough won at bools and he swopped Shuggy Clelland for his Captain Marvel comics; well Shuggy gave it to me for a loan of my gider for a week.’
‘So!’ said Ewan.
‘Well, I had to try it out to make sure that it worked.’
‘Really.’ commented Matt. ‘My dad wouldn’t have let me carve my initials on the toilet seat.’
‘Neither did my dad.’ I admitted honestly.
‘You mean your mum and dad don’t know,’ piped up Ronnie.
‘Will you all hurry up and finish,’ I said ‘and let’s get out of here; the girls are waiting desperately.’
‘When will your dad know?’ asked Matt.
‘When I leave to join the army,’ I said.
I locked the door and ushered the boys back into the house

where I handed the key over to Isobel and the girls who for some reason or another were all standing with their legs crossed. 'You don't need to lift the seat,' I said, ignoring the funny look she gave me.
'Has everybody been to the toilet before I hang up the key?' asked mum as the girls returned into the house. 'Are we all sure now? 'Howard, it's your turn at the piano again. Some nice quiet carols for the children to sing please.'
'Right,' said dad sitting down on the stool and lifting the piano lid and off we went again;
'Silent Night, Holy Night.' followed by 'Away in a Manger.' Everyone joined in singing as sweetly as they could and from the bottom of their hearts. Little ones who were nodding over were placed on a quilt near the Christmas tree and tucked up together with a blanket over them. The older children talked, laughed and amused themselves by discussing what Santa would bring them when he called during the night and what food they were going to leave out for his and Rudolph's supper.
'How about the 'Toorie on his Bonnet,' shouted Jeanie and off the adults went into full vocal swing.
Everyone knew the words and it was followed by 'Bonnie Dundee', 'Scotland The Brave', 'Cherry Ripe', 'Cruising Down The River' and mum's own favourite, 'Jeannie With The Light brown Hair'.
Old Elly who had been sitting quietly enjoying the company and the happy atmosphere around the fire requested a song but as she couldn't remember the words, she started humming the tune. Within seconds everyone joined in:
'With someone like you, a pal so good and true,' a tear rolled down Elly's cheek; it must have been past memories and that second sherry having an effect. She lived on her own across the landing and often came over to mums for company in the evenings when Isobel or Mary would sit by the fire and brush her hair which was long enough for her to sit on. She kept it up and in a bun during the day and only let it down to be brushed or when going to bed. I once heard mum say that she always kept some chocolate in her kitchen drawer for children who went to the shops for the odd message or two for her and I remember her giving

me a few squares.
'I'd like to leave it all behind and go and find,' sang Granny Reader who was Isobel and Mary's Granny.
'That's it,' shouted Elly.
'A real favourite it is too,' shouted Granny Reader who was stone deaf in both ears which wasn't helped by her hearing aid in one ear continually falling out.
All join in the last line; shouted dad 'And let the rest of the world go by.' Cheers and clapping all round which didn't even raise a whimper from the children deep in the land of fairytales, Santa Clause and Nod.
'We'll follow that one up shouted dad, with 'The Boys of the old Brigade.'
'Mind your feet stamping on the floor,' called mum; ever thoughtful about Old Corky down below.
'He'll be sleeping by now,' someone shouted.
'Not for long,' was the reply.
'Right boys, shoes off and we'll march quietly,' said dad and once more, off we went in full swing accompanied by the piano, the accordion and the mouth organ; not to mention all the actions of marching and saluting up and down the floor.
How the night ended, I cannot remember but as everyone went home smiling and laughing, it must have been a happy night. Everyone wished everyone else a Merry Christmas and thanked mum and dad for a wonderful evening; one that everyone would remember.
I was sure dad would remember to extinguish the fire before Santa slithered down the chimney and put the consequences of him forgetting, out of my mind but I did cross my fingers as added insurance.
On Christmas morning we made a snowman, had snowball fights and sledged down the pavements of Grove Street. Dad had to go to work like many dads in Scotland but promised to try and get home early for our Christmas meal. It was still snowing.

Chapter 30 - Christmas Morning

On Christmas morning, we awoke early.
'Did you see him?' Eleanor asked, pushing the cover aside and sitting up in her bed.
'I did,' said Ally, 'he was tiptoeing to the bowl of food that we left for Rudolph beside the fireplace.'
'Wow!!' Said Eleanor and pulled the blanket back over her head.
Ally shook me and we peered down to the end of the double bed which we shared, to see if Santa had filled the pillow slips left hanging there on Christmas Eve and he had. Eleanor heard our gasps of excitement and popped up. 'Did Santa leave me anything?' she asked.
'No, sorry he's missed you,' I said teasing her.
'I'm telling mum,' she screamed.
'Right, all right,' I said, my voice rising to blank out her scream before she woke mum and dad who were sleeping in the wee room next door. 'I was only kidding.' The screaming stopped.
The five stockings hanging up on the string line above the fireplace were bulging. The contents of three included an apple, an orange, sweets, a lollypop and some small goodies which were all emptied on to the floor amongst the other presents. The next two hours were spent sitting on the floor ripping off the Christmas wrapping paper and playing with the new toys and even the empty boxes that had contained presents a few moments before. I had a football annual, an adventure book, football socks, a Hearts football scarf, jigsaw puzzle, a snakes and ladders board game, a Dinky Car and a mechano set. We sat amongst the discarded wrappings showing each other our presents and were lost in a magic world of our own. Most years, I would get a copy of The Broons Annual and Ally would get Oor Wullie which allowed us to read and swap.

The other two stockings on the line contained favourite titbits for Dopey the cat and Nelly the budgie.
'Merry Christmas,' cried, mum and dad as they entered the room, 'Hope Santa was good to you and gave you most of what you had asked for in your letter to him.'
'Yes he did,' we all shouted at the top of our voices.
'Merry Christmas mum and dad,' said Ally.
'Merry Christmas, mum and dad,' Eleanor and I echoed Ally.
'Santa has left a present for each of you,' said Eleanor bubbling with excitement, 'they're under the Christmas tree.'
'That was very nice of him.' replied dad. 'I've got to go to work now but I'll open mine at our Christmas dinner to-night. 'I'll try to finish early.'
'I'll open mine right now,' said mum as she moved towards the Christmas tree peering under the bottom branches. 'I hope that you three haven't been guzzling too many sweets and I think that we should put all that paper back into one bag and tidy up the floor before breakfast. We must remember those children not as lucky as you are but we'll talk about that later.'
Mum loved her new apron and woollen gloves and thanked all three of us for asking Santa to deliver such lovely presents to her. 'Did you notice, that the warm milk and biscuits you left for Rudolph had gone and have you read the note lying here?' she asked bending down to the empty bowl and picking up a bit of paper. 'Shall I read what it says?'
'Oh please,' said Eleanor.
'Dear children,' read mum, 'thank-you very much for Rudolph's supper. He especially enjoyed the warm milk on this very cold and wintry night and he did share the shortbread with me. It was scrumptious. I hope that you will be happy with your presents and do have a very happy Christmas. Lots of love, from Santa; must fly, lots of presents to deliver before the children waken up; 'Ho! Ho! Ho! I'm off now. Merry Christmas.'
We looked at each other and looked back at the note in mum's hand. We still believed in Santa just in case we

didn't get any presents.
Like many men, dad had to work on Christmas Day and had the holiday at New Year but he had promised to try and get home early for our Christmas meal.
After breakfast mum reminded us of the children with no mums or dads and who lived in special homes. 'As in the past,' she said, 'we should try to take them a present at this special time of the year.' Isobel and Mary joined us, each holding a small present. 'Right!' said mum 'Get wrapped up and let's be on our way before it snows again.' We put on our warm clothing, coats, gloves, scarves, balaclavas, warm socks and last of all at the door, our welly boots. As agreed we each selected a present to give to the children and as guided by mum, it was something that they could share and enjoy together such as a jigsaw puzzle or a game and mum picked up from the sideboard a box of chocolates for members of the staff. We set off down Grove Street and up Morrison Street, trudging through the snow which had continued falling during the night. We passed the Regal Cinema turned right for Tolcross, through the meadows and up the slope to the children's home at Marchment. Ally rang the bell outside a huge green door which was opened by a smiling, grey haired lady wearing a blue uniform and a white apron.
'You will have come to see the children,' she said as she opened the door wider. 'Come away in. You are so very welcome, the children don't get many visitors and to-day is very special.' She led us down the long hall and opened a door marked playroom. There was an awkward silence as the children stopped playing and looked up at the strangers entering their room but it wasn't long before their faces were beaming all over as they jumped up, took our hands and guided us over to see their Christmas tree. We were accepted by them and within no time at all we were playing and laughing with them as if we had known them all our lives.
Time passed quickly and as we left, they crowded around the front door waving and shouting, 'thank-you for your lovely presents.'
'Santa didn't come to our house and we didn't see

Rudolph,' said one little girl with a very sad look on her face.
'He was very busy last night,' said mum, 'I'm sure that he will pop in next year.'
'Will you please come and see us again?' she pleaded with her hands clasped in front of her.
'We will,' we promised. It seemed the right thing to say at the time, 'Merry Christmas,' we shouted as we left them on the doorstep waving goodbye to us.
'I wished we could take them all home with us,' said mum as she wiped away a tear which was rolling down her cheek.
'We are so lucky,' said Isobel leaning over to give mum a cuddle and taking her arm.
'Let's go home and have our Christmas Dinner,' said mum.
'Aye!' we all shouted.
As we made our way back between the Meadows and the Links where children were sledging on the slopes, frolicking in the snow, making snowmen and enjoying snowball fights, I thought that we were all thinking of less fortunate children.
It's snowing again,' shouted Eleanor. We all looked up to see large flakes meandering down to land on our hats and on the path around us.
Mary smiled, 'It really is Christmas,' she said 'and a lovely morning for Jesus to have been born.'
Dad did make it home early. Mum had prepared a large steak pie with all the trimmings and the aroma emanating from the kitchen was truly mouth-watering. Even with three children sitting on the coal bunker the kitchen was too small and mum had set the table in the big room. Isobel, Mary, their mum and old Elly joined us and all nine of us sat down together to say grace.
When the pie was cut open, the steam arose and the piping hot beef popped up shimmering beneath the crisp brown pastry. The meal was dished up on to the plates with the adults all helping to
serve the roast potatoes and vegetables. Dad served up individually the piping hot gravy.
With paper hats on our heads, we pulled the crackers,

taking it in turns to read out the jokes and tried to find the little favours that scattered all over the place when the crackers opened with the customary bang. Dad opened his present and with a huge beam on his face, thanked us all for the Heart's maroon tie and the pair of warm bed socks.
The noise of chatter and laughter only stopped when dad carried in the plum duff Christmas pudding with a sprig of holly on top, poured some brandy over it and struck a match. It was awe inspiring to see the blue flames curling up and around the holly. It was the custom for silver threepenny bits to be dispersed amongst the currants, raisons and mixed spicy fruits of the pudding and was considered to be good luck for those who found them in their helpings. Once they had been retrieved delicious creamola was poured over the pudding on the plates and we all tucked in. After the sweets and nuts, a glass of sherry was poured for the adults although dad had a wee dram instead. We children helped to clear the table and wash and dry the dishes under the auspices of Isobel who was the oldest and seemed to know how to organise cleaning and washing up. The adults retired to sit in front of the fire, half snoozing, enjoying the company and the warmth of the night.
'Well,' asked dad, when we children had joined the adults, 'did you enjoy taking your presents up to the children in the home?'
'Yes,' we all shouted
'And did it make you realise how lucky you are?'
'Yes,' we replied rather sadly.
'It was very sad having to leave them,' Isobel said quietly 'but I think that we helped to make them happy.'
'I know that you did,' said dad. 'Well done to you all.'
'It's still snowing,' said Jeanie.
Dad held out his arms and beckoned to us. 'Let's snuggle closer to the fire,' he said, 'I think I have a story that you will all enjoy.'

Chapter 31 - I Was Brave

Mum and dad were always encouraging us at the table to eat our food up. 'Clear your plate,' they would say, 'there are lots of black babies in Africa who would be glad of it.' Dad would bring home a ham shank from the St. Cuthbert's grocery department where he worked and mum adding lentils, barley and split peas would make a lovely pot of soup. Although scotch broth full of vegetables was deemed healthy, the sight of a whole sheep's heid or a flank of mutton going into the pot was not so appetising but tattie soup made with a marrowbone was cheap, nourishing, wholesome and popular.
After ox tongue soup, the whole tongue would be laid out on a plate and sliced up for the main course. 'Ugh!' We were encouraged to drink the water in which the cabbage had been boiled in, to keep our bowls open; often it flushed right through. Tripe which was a cow's stomach and potted haugh were very cheap but again not very popular. Other standard dishes were stovies (mashed tatties with pieces of sausage or meat with onions), corn beef, faggots, varieties of fish and cod roe accompanied by vegetables such as turnips leeks onions, carrots, beans, peas, sprouts, cabbage and cauliflower. Mince and tatties, haggis, fish and chips were among the most popular foods. A Finnan Haddie (Finnan Haddock) was a real treat and sardines and pilchards were tasty on toast. The Newhaven fishwives in their distinct black shawls and headscarves, carrying on their backs, their laden baskets of fresh fish and mussels were very popular with the folks of Edinburgh. A strap around their foreheads and attached to the baskets supported their backs when walking around the streets to set up their regular stalls at street corners.
Lettuce, sliced carrots, cucumbers, tomatoes, sybies (spring onions] and boiled eggs were made up into salads

and although very healthy were not top of the choice list. Although long narrow empty boxes with Fyffe's Bananas stamped on the side lay outside Rankin's fruit shop awaiting collection we never had bananas at home.
Breakfast was usually porridge, weetabix or cornflakes, boiled eggs, rolls or toast with margarine, marmalade, lemon curd, jam or syrup. If we were very lucky on a Sunday, we might get a fried egg, streaky bacon, black pudding and a sausage accompanied with a dripping piece [bread dipped in fat from the frying pan). Apples, oranges and rhubarb with the end dipped in sugar were popular and at times pomegranates, plums, gooseberries, raspberries and strawberries sometimes appeared on the table with the odd grapefruit, pineapple or grapes. Hazelnuts, almonds, walnuts and monkey nuts seemed to be present on festive occasions only.
Puddings were usually rice with milk, bread and butter pudding, rhubarb crumble or cake and custard which often had a thick skin on it unlike creamola.
Our family doctor was Doctor Dodson who was a large rotund gentleman, balding with a bristling moustache and glasses. He always wore a jacket and tie and kept a stethoscope with other medical instruments to hand on a small compact writing bureau. He had a welcoming manner and underneath his moustache there was usually a hint of a smile. He took a pride in remembering our names as if he were an uncle in the family. On one occasion when I was violently sick, mum thought that I had caught a bug and walked me up to the doctor's surgery which was near the Kings Theatre up from Tolcross. After examining me the doctor handed me a long glass and asked if I could pass him some water. Taking the glass I went to the small sink, filled the glass with water and handed it back to the doctor who looked at me and smiled. My mother was mortified. 'You've always got to misbehave Howard. I'm fair affronted and I don't know what the doctor thinks of us. I do apologise doctor,'
'Not at all Mrs Gee, I'm sure young Howard will pop into the toilet closet there and do me a wee piddle into the glass,' and I did.

'Thank you Howard. That's a good boy. We'll soon see if you have an infection. I'll let your mother know as soon as possible.'
'Thank goodness we don't have to bother the doctor too much,' mum said one day nodding towards the full shelf in the cupboard containing caster and cod liver oils, liquid paraffin, milk of magnesia which was dad's favourite remedy for everything. Worm powders, syrup of figs, Andrews Liver Salts and dark brown malt which was one of the more pleasant medicines that rolled off the spoon on to our tongues. Varieties of cough mixtures including ipecacuonha wine, iodine for burning off warts, warm almond oil for sore ears, toothache tincture, and valderma for the dreaded spots that seemed to be part of the growing up process were all on the shelf. Menthol crystals cleared blocked noses and throats as the patient sat over a basin with a towel on their head which dropped between their knees; allowing the vapour to rise up the nose. It did work but it didn't half make your eyes water. Dettol made the bravest of the brave wince whilst antiseptic cream, elastoplasts and small pieces of lint, swabs and bandages were invaluable.
I once had on my right foot, a poisoned big toe which was very red and swollen. Mum made a poultice comprised of bread, sugar and grated soap mixed into a paste with boiled milk and spread on to a piece of lint gauze to draw out the poison; a bandage held it in place. To get my shoe on I had to force my foot into it causing a bulge in the leather. After a bit of throbbing and sobbing the poison oozed out with a welcomed relief but my shoe was never the same again during the rest of my shoe life. Jimmy Brough asked me if I had a boil growing in my sock. I ignored him.
I do remember my mother one day, discussing with a neighbour the dangers of us children playing in the old cellars of the stair and the fear that all parents had of their children catching chicken pox ,diphtheria or scarlet fever and something about the big killer tuberculosis more commonly known as T.B.
At school the nurse came round inspecting the hair and

scalp for nits [beasties) and took the opportunity to look for any signs of impetigo usually showing up on one's face and was considered to be attracted from dirty locations. The unfortunate few who contacted it, had blue jenson violet dabbed on to the infectious areas which lit up like a beacon for the whole school to see. Picking one's nose was very much frowned on especially if sooking one's finger after it. I dreaded the nurse asking me to take off my shirt to examine me as mum always insisted that I wore a long woolly vest with a round neck, three buttons down the front and short sleeves. It didn't seem to worry other children including girls in the class and it certainly didn't bother mum.

When mumps appeared you wore a scarf under your chin and tied it on the top of your head to help keep the swelling in your cheeks down by keeping them warm. For measles which were highly contagious, you had to stay at home under the doctor's orders whilst scarlet fever was a very serious infection and required a stay in hospital. The arrival of penicillin along with inoculations against diphtheria and poliomyelitis gave children a better chance of a healthy childhood as compared to our parent's day. Unfortunately, I proved to be allergic to penicillin

One night I woke up crying with toothache and mum managed to deaden the pain with a toothache tincture but the following morning it had got worse again. At first I thought great news, I can't go to school; then I realised that dad had said that I would have to go to the dentist before school. It was raining, I had toothache and as mum walked me down to the dentist at Haymarket, I thought to myself how miserable life was. It just wasn't fair.

The door of the waiting room opened and I heard the receptionist's voice, 'come away through Mrs Gee the dentist will see Howard now.'

'Pop up on the chair young man,' said the dentist. 'Don't be frightened now, I'm just going to press the button and let the chair slip backwards to allow me to have a good look and find the cause of the trouble'

Peering and prodding in my mouth the dentist reviewed the situation and decided that the faulty tooth would have to

come out. I shut my eyes, hunched my shoulders and took a sharp intake of breath. I wondered if it would be easier to tie a thread from my tooth to the door handle and shut the door but I'd have to find someone to shut the door. Ally would willingly have helped but he would have slammed it shut. 'The pain, oh the pain,' I thought to myself.
'If you would just retire to the waiting room Mrs Gee,' requested the dentist rubbing his hands, looking at me and smiling. 'I'll look after young Howard here.' I looked up at mum with big spaniel like eyes pleading not to be left on my own but I was too much of a man to say anything. Seeing that I was about to make a run for it, the dentist bent down, held my chin and looked into my mouth. You'll be fine Howard and we'll get rid of that nasty old tooth causing you that nasty pain.
'I'll just be next door in the waiting room Howard,' called mum as she disappeared out of the room.
The female assistant wearing a white apron pushed a small round table on wheels towards me. I was aghast and held my breath at seeing the tray full of chisels, pliers and levers and only removed my eyes when a large round light was pulled down from above to almost touch my face.
'Just breathe into the bag Howard,' she said, holding up what looked like a football bladder. As she placed the bag over my mouth and nose, she held my hand and asked me in a soft voice if I was a Hearts or Hibs supporter.
'What does she know about football?' I thought to myself 'and she's not going to get me to go to sleep anyway.' I was now feeling drowsy and struggling to keep my eyes open; drifting into a deep sleep.
'Just relax Howard,' I heard her voice whispering softly in my ear and that was the last that I heard. I was floating in a land of dreams.
'Open your eyes now but just relax and lie still.' A man's voice was reaching into the ramblings of my mind. My eye lids parted and I tried to leap off the chair which was moving to the upright position when a firm hand on my shoulder held me down. I couldn't focus on where I was until my tongue touched a large piece of swabbing in my gum and I jerked into the real world.

'Would you like to keep your tooth?' asked the assistant showing it to me in a piece of cotton wool. 'You can put it under your pillow tonight and maybe the Tooth Fairy will leave you a silver coin.'
'Does she still believe in Tooth Fairies?' I asked myself, although it just might work. 'Yes please,' I said politely.
'Oh, that's nice,' she said. 'Now if you would just rinse your mouth out, there's a cup at your left hand side. Swirl it around your mouth and spit it into the basin,' which I did and watched as the gurgling water carried my mouthful of spit and blood away down the small plug hole. I think that I spat too hard as I heard her say, 'oh dear, never mind, I'll mop the floor.' She took me through to the waiting room where my mother gave me an embarrassing hug in front of the other patients who looked on and smiled.
'Perhaps you would like to sit a few minutes with your mother Howard before going down the stairs to the front door. They are quite steep. Would you like to go to the toilet first?'
'What did she say?' I asked myself knowing that my face was beetroot red.
'It's just outside on the left,' she said pointing her finger.
Everyone in the waiting room was still looking at me and smiling.
What a relief to get down the stairs, outside and be heading for home.
I didn't tell the boys that I placed my tooth under my pillow but mum gave me sixpence for being so brave and that, I did tell the boys.

Chapter 32 - Our Hoose

Although we didn't think much about it, home was a front facing top flat in Grove Street. The key rested in the lock and usually when turned and the door opened a breath of warm air from the coal fire wafted out and welcomed all who stepped inside. Coats were hung up in the lobby which led through to the big room but a left turn led to the glory hole and the small kitchen which was the hub of the house.
Behind the kitchen door was the sink where the only source of water into the house came from the cold water tap. With the aid of hot water from the large black kettle that sat continuously on the coal fire, socks, handkerchiefs, underwear and small items of clothing were washed, rinsed and hung up to dry on the string line which stretched below the mantel piece and above the fire. As there was no room to stack dirty dishes, they were washed at the sink straight after meals, dried and put away in their respective drawers and cupboards.
On non-bath nights which were most nights of the week, we stood in the sink whilst our bodies, knees and feet had lifebuoy or coal tar soap applied and scrubbed with a stiff brush. Our hair was washed in warm water from the kettle and rinsed under the cold tap.
When mum wasn't in the house football boots and anything else needing cleaned were rinsed through under the tap and hidden out of the way in the glory hole amongst the tools, stepladders, brushes, buckets, mops, pots of paint, turpentine and anything else that had to be stored somewhere, not to mention Dopey the cat who had freedom of movement through a small window leading out on to the lobby. Once all windows were checked in the evenings, Nelly the budgie was allowed out of her cage to fly around the kitchen where everyone would converse with

her as if she was a member of the family.
Meals were in the kitchen and the table was lifted over to the coalbunker where three children could sit comfortably. There was no fridge and all foods were kept along with cups, saucers, plates and cutlery neatly stored in the cupboard next to the coalbunker. Although the bread bin and biscuit tins gave some protection when the coalmen tipped their one hundred weight bags of coal into the bunker, coal dust rose and reached every nook and cranny. Whoever had designed the house way back in time had obviously not associated coal dust and cupboards with questionable hygiene but we never thought to reason why mum was always washing and cleaning out shelves and telling us to keep the cupboard door and coal bunker lid closed.
The bread was normally a plain half loaf which had to be cut into slices on the bread board with a long sharp breadknife; each slice having one black crust and one more popular brown crust at the other end. One day we had just arrived home from school when Ally my younger brother by eighteen months said that he was starving and decided to make a piece on jam but whilst slicing the bread he unfortunately sliced his fingers with the breadknife. There was weeping and wailing with blood everywhere. I was trying to get him to stand still while I wrapped a bandage around his fingers when mum walked in. The tempo was raised immediately to screeching and shouting at me for letting Ally use a breadknife; after all he was my younger brother and I should have known better.
Mum took charge of the situation, wrapped a dish towel around the bandage and led Ally downstairs with real tears rolling down his cheeks.
'Howard, you stay and try to clean up that blood until we get back and keep out of trouble.'
'Right mum,' I shouted as I watched her from the window leading Ally down the street and across to the chemist shop in Morrison Street where the gash was assessed and dressed. The chemist advised mum that a few stitches would be needed. A number two bus took mum and Ally up to the Royal Infirmary and a few hours later, both were

safely home and all was well. Ally had three stitches in his fingers. I had set the table, started my homework and was trying hard not to be seen and although by this time, I was starving, I hadn't dared to think of having a piece on jam and anyway the loaf had blood all over it. When he came in from work, dad had the whole story related to him before he even had time to take off his cap and hang his jacket on the peg in the lobby.

'I hope that you have learned a lesson,' he said, looking sternly at Ally and me 'and that you must be very careful in future especially when using sharp knives.'

'Yes dad, we have and we will.'

Ally looked at me and said, 'sorry Howard,' and both of us looked across the table and said, 'sorry mum and thank-you,'

Everything that happened in the kitchen was generally centred on the fireplace especially in the evenings when the leaping fingers of flames from the burning coals beckoned all to come and sit around. The family and neighbours made toast taking turns to hold the bread on the long brass toasting fork out in front of the fire. Isobel, Mary, their mum and old Elly were in the house most nights and dad who was the best story teller would only begin when everyone was sitting comfortably by the fire, usually with a mug of cocoa to accompany the hot buttered toast. As we stared into the warm beckoning fire, crackling sparks, like tiny shooting stars shot up the lum from the burning coals, and characters from dad's tales came to life. We sat, until we children started yawning which heralded in mum's call; 'time for bed.'

Mum on her hands and knees kept the linoleum on the floor polished but we were always alert for any small pieces of coal that had jumped out of the fire on to the linoleum or the small rug that sat in front of the fireplace. Large lumps of coal were broken up in the bunker and carried over on the shovel to stoke up the fire. Kept inside the bunker was the hammer, shovel, axe, bundles of firewood, firelighters and old newspapers for kindling the fire.

Around the fireplace was a brass fender with a stool at

each end and a seat which served as a lid. Inside the stools were kept varieties of brushes for cleaning anything that needed cleaned. Tins of zeebo for blackening and cleaning the grate, shoe polish, floor polish, dusters, tins of brasso and odds and ends which didn't have a storage place of their own. A poker, tongs and small Bellows' used for getting the fire started lay on the hearth.

Never far away was mum's large tin box which had all her sewing and repair materials such as needles, thimbles, varieties of buttons, reels of thread, coloured wool, safety pins ,scissors and darning wool. A wooden mushroom which was placed inside a jersey or a sock beneath the hole to be darned, gave support for the criss crossing of the wool over the hole. Various types of leather materials were used to patch some items of clothing such as the rear end of trousers or elbows on the sleeves of pullovers.

Off the kitchen was the wee room where mum and dad managed to have a double bed, chest of drawers and a small wooden chair squeezed in to it. Back in the lobby which led to the big room, the shoes, boots and wellies were lined up underneath the coats hanging on the pegs. Hanging above the main door was a set of bull's horns sticking out from a black furry centre piece where the head would normally have been. It had just always hung there. Throughout the winter afternoons and on special evenings the fire was lit in the big room where four large windows looked down on to our street. Mum always had an afternoon pot of tea with a neighbour or a friend around three o'clock and on most occasions there was a biscuit and a warm drink waiting for us when we arrived home from school.

The baby grand piano nestled into the corner of the room with the settee and arm chairs placed strategically around the fire to allow everyone to share the warmth. When Eleanor outgrew her cot, it was replaced by a single bed.

Family photographs sat on the bookcase and as adults talked about life in general, dad would often play the piano as we children read books, made up jig saws or played with games quietly in front of the fire.

Although it wasn't always appreciated, it was generally

happy times in our home.
We lived cheek by jowl with our neighbours in the stair and the street. Everyone knew each other, cared for one another in times of need and could be relied on to help when required. Differences were forgotten quickly or so it all seemed to us children who just wanted to play and enjoy life.

Chapter 33 - Teamwork

To get school out of our systems, the week-ends had to be enjoyed to the full and Portobello outdoor pool was a popular choice by the gang. Even on the hottest of days the salt water pool was cold and although the pool was often packed, most people were not swimming but lying around the sides talking and sunbathing.
The great attraction of the pool was the waves. When they came on at regular intervals, most bathers jumped into the water and as the waves got higher and higher, bobbing heads appeared briefly before disappearing beneath the surface again. Although it never crossed our minds, the mingling crowds of floating, moving bodies, laughing, shouting and screaming must have been a lifeguard's nightmare but we were never aware of the danger and loved the thrill of the waves. There was a very high diving board and those of us who dared to jump from it, gained respect from our pals.
'If I dive it, will you have a go?' asked Bobby, looking daringly at me as we sat on the edge of the pool looking up at the board.
'What?'
'Come on Howard, we can do it.'
'Do what?' asked Shuggy as Mac, Ewan and Matt listened intently.
'Dive off the high dive,' stressed Bobby irritated that we hadn't got the jist of what he was talking about.
'What!!' I said again.'
'Right, I'm going to do it myself,' said Bobby indignantly as he strode off to the far side of the pool via the deep end.
'You can't do it when the waves are on,' Matt said trying to look sensible.
I looked at him, 'they're not on,' I said wishing that they were.

'Y'er daft, and yer faither will kill you if the water disnae,' shouted Mac shaking his head.
'Och! Right, I'm going to have a go,' and plucking up courage from the souls of my feet, I ran after Bobby.
'No running.' came the voice of the vigilant lifeguard holding up his megaphone for all to see; no doubt feeling good that he had spotted someone breaking the rules.
'We'll watch from here,' said Matt.
After ages and ages of climbing up the steps, we reached the top diving board. I looked over the edge at the tiny swimmers below and felt sick. What a stupid idea this was I thought to myself.
'Don't worry Howard, the diving area is roped off, you won't hurt anyone when you land,' Bobby said very calmly.
'I wasn't thinking of anyone else getting hurt, I was thinking of me,' I replied.
'Oh,' said Bobby, I never thought about that. I'll go first anyway.'
'Oh, no, I'll go first,' I said 'you're not going to leave me up here on my own.'
'You'll be alright, take a deep breath and just go for it,' said Bobby. 'Are you doing a straight or a tuck dive?'
'Just head first,' I answered.
'Are you sure?'
'Course I am'
'Right,' I said, getting my dander up seeing the four lads waving and making rude gestures at me from across the pool. 'I'm not walking down those stairs.'
'Go on then,' said Bobby, stepping back to make room for me.
I stood with my toes over the edge of the board, looked straight ahead, shut my eyes and fell forwards. My arms without any help from me, spread sideways into the swallow position as down I plunged into the waiting dark watery abyss. I felt my head thump, my spine jar on impact and I tried to push up from the bottom but my feet hadn't reached it. Frantically I kicked and splashed my way upwards like a snowman trying desperately to get away from a bonfire. My head broke the surface and as I gulped in large breaths of fresh air, I was disappointed not to see

the crowds standing around the pool cheering and clapping with autograph books in their hands.
I looked up and saw Bobby hurtling down like a hen harrier after its prey. There was a mighty splash, a few yards to my right before a smiling face popped up a few seconds later.
'Yes,' we shouted, throwing our arms up in the air as if we had just visited Davy Jones's locker and arrived safely back again. We climbed out and there were the lads waiting.
'Did you change your mind and jump instead of diving?' asked Matt.
Before we could reach him, Matt assured us that he was only kidding and admitted that we were daft but very brave to have done it.
'Aye,' the other three agreed.
'Well, we'll never do it again,' said Bobby 'but could you please tell everyone at school how brave we were.'
The rest of the day was spent performing crazy antics from the spring board into the pool. On the way home we ate our shivery bites on the top deck of the bus where the conductor couldn't see us.
'You were terrific Bobby.'
'So were you Howard.'
'Ugh!!' said the lads and we all burst out laughing.
Some Sundays we would cycle to Cramond, roll in the sand, play football or just enjoy running into the sea for a swim and a splash about. As we couldn't leave our bicycles unattended, we didn't walk out to Cramond Island and were always glad that we hadn't when we saw the rescue teams being called out to rescue those who had misjudged the tide and had become stranded.
Once cycling home from Gullane, we passed by the wooden huts at Port Seaton Camp and decided to buy some flounders at the nearby harbour to take home to our mums as a surprise. We bought one each and tied them together with a piece of string. It was agreed that I would fasten the string to my cycle bag attached to the rear of my seat. As we cycled through the busy main street of Musselburgh, a huge cattle truck passed us travelling in

the opposite direction and in its slipstream, I knew that something had come off my bike. I shouted to the lads and we all pulled over into the side. The string had snapped and the flounders were slithering about under the passing traffic. We looked at each other, shrugged our shoulders, jumped on our bikes and headed for home. Nothing more was said about the flounders for a week or two until one day, remembering the incident, we all had a good laugh.

On occasions we would cycle to South Queensferry to catch the Saint Margaret's Ferry across the Forth and cycle on to Dunfermline Abbey where we would have our snacks in the park as the peacocks strutted around us. On the way home, cycling up the Hawse Brae after disembarking from the ferry was always a real challenge to see who could reach the top without having to lift ones behind off the seat. It was ages before I managed it.

When the Union Canal iced over in the winter, it was a favourite attraction for children to slide on it in spite of the obvious danger of falling through the ice. We never thought nor worried about it and would walk or slide across from bank to bank especially when dared to do it.

Lads from other streets would sometimes appear and throw stones at the ice around us, running off before we could climb up the bank to catch them. Stones thrown at water rats on the opposite bank, never reached them; they just skidded across the ice until they came to a halt. I don't think that the rats were ever aware or even bothered about missiles heading in their direction.

One dull drizzly afternoon Billy Macleod, his brother Jimmy and I, on a mission of adventure were walking on the tow path under the bridge near Harrison Park, when we heard a woman's voice shouting for someone to help her. As we rounded some bushes on our right we saw that her dog had ran away from her. The wee Cairn Terrier had jumped on to the ice, scrambled over to the middle and fell through into the cold water of the canal. All we could see was a little head bobbing up through the hole in the ice and giving a whimper before disappearing again. Without thinking Billy hurtled down the bank, on to the ice and started running out to the dog.

'What's his name?' I asked the woman who by now was screaming at the top of her voice and pointing at the hole in the ice.
'Winston,' she shouted.
Jimmy and I stepped on to the ice warily, shouting to Billy that the dog's name was Winston.
As Billy reached the hole, he lay flat and outstretched his right hand. Winston's little head popped up again and Billy grabbed his collar and hoicked him out of the hole.
'Easy, good boy Winston,' I said as Billy tried to keep hold of his wriggling wet body whilst yapping and licking his face. Billy passed him to me and I handed him to Jimmy who stuffed Winston inside his jerkin and walked slowly back to the bank where his mistress could hardly contain herself; jumping up and down with joy. She didn't mind at all getting soaking wet as she cuddled and hugged her wee Winston.
'Well done,' I said to Billy in a grown up way not foreseeing the danger of the cracking ice beneath us and as through the ice he went, he grabbed the sleeve of my jumper pulling me through the hole with him. We heard the woman on the bank let out an almighty scream and out of the corner of my eye, I saw a man running along the towpath towards us carrying a rope with a lifebelt tied to the end of it; these were positioned at intervals along the path.
'I'm coming lads,' he shouted, 'hold on.'
Billy looked at me; 'are we going to drown?' he asked
'I don't think so, my feet are touching the bottom.'
'So are mine,' whispered Billy as the truth began to sink in. We stood up to our waist in the frozen Union Canal and burst out laughing.
'It's freezing,' I said. 'Let's get out of here. I don't suppose you've got ice skates with you?'
'How did you know that?' asked Billy sarcastically.
The newcomer, who turned out to be a council worker, had been repairing the swings at the nearby park when he heard the commotion. Holding the rope, he slid the lifebelt over the ice towards us. The cracks in the ice were getting bigger as we grabbed the belt and the man assisted by Jimmy heaved on the rope and we slid along the ice back

to the bank and safety.
'Oh thanks,' we shouted as we clambered out of the water and stood shivering. It was only then that I spotted the helmet and the blue uniform.
'Where are you lads from?' enquired the policeman in that policeman like tone 'and what have you been up to?'
'Grove Street sir and we haven't been doing anything,'
'That's a fair way down the road,' said the policeman with a doubtful look on his face.
'My name is Mrs Mathews officer and these young men have saved my wee Winston from drowning. They are indeed real heroes.'
'Aye said the council worker brave lads they are indeed.'
'May I ask your name sir as I may require a statement from you later on?' said the constable
'John Scott and you can find me at the Council Yard just over the back.' he said pointing his finger in the direction of the yard.
'Thank-you sir. Right! Let's get you young lads over to the police box,' he said, pointing with his chin towards the park entrance. 'You're obviously very wet and beginning to look a bit blue. There's a couple of towels in the box and I'll give you a hot drink and see if we can get you a ride home in the police van. I'd be grateful Mrs Mathews if you would call into the police box later to-day and give me the full story for my report.'
'I will constable,' and she turned to Winston, now firmly on his lead; 'Winston say thank-you and cheerio to the boys.' Winston Barked twice and we looked at each other in disbelief. 'Thank-you again boys,' and with a wave of her hand, she went off along the canal bank.
'I'm sure your mother will understand about your lost shoe,' said P.C. Bell to Billy who looked down at his left shoeless foot.
'Oh no,' cried Billy, 'it's my school shoe.'
'Well we're not going back in for it,' I said.
'I'll mention it to Mrs Mathews,' the policeman said, 'perhaps she'll explain the situation to your mother.' The Black Maria duly arrived and took us home in style.
The following day, Mrs, Mathews turned up at Grove Street

and related the full story to our mothers over a cup of tea. She explained how we had saved her wee Winston, the only loved one she had left in the whole world and that he was still sleeping the nasty experience off, even now in his warm doggie bed at home.
She had asked our mums to thank us all again and when we arrived home from school, to our delight, she had left us each a large bag of mixed boilings and had given Billy's mother two pounds to buy him a new pair of school shoes.

Chapter 34 - Mischief

One sunny Saturday morning after breakfast, we gathered on the front stairs outside the tenement in Grove Street. Billy Macleod, Ronnie Nesbit, Jimmy Brough and I were contemplating what we should do that day.
'I've got three pence on me,' I said. 'Anyone else got pocket money on them?'
'I have and me too,' echoed Ronnie and Billy together.
'I've only got two pence.' said Jimmy with a pathetic wee voice.
'I'll lend you a penny,' said Billy very generously.
'You owe me a penny from two weeks ago.' Replied Jimmy emphatically
'I don't remember that.'
'I do,' answered Jimmy. 'We came out of Dalry Baths, went for chips and you didn't have any money.'
'Oh aye, yer right,' Interrupted Billy.
'In that case we have the funds to cross over to the bakers shop and buy a wagon wheel each,' I said; which we did. Sitting back on the stairs again, tucking into our biscuits with chocolate all over our mouths and fingers, we had to suddenly move to let Mrs Dobbie down the stairs with her large pram and chortling baby inside.
'What are you boys up to this morning?' she asked, with a hint of suspicion in her voice.
'Nothing, Mrs Dobbie. Can we help you down the stairs with your pram?'
'Thank you very much for offering boys but I'll just bump it down. The last time you helped, Amelia nearly bounced out of the pram. Now you boys keep out of mischief,' she called as she successfully manoeuvred the pram down the last few stairs and on to the pavement. 'Remember what I'm saying now,' she shouted, looking back over her right shoulder as she wheeled her pram down the hill.

We had just sat down on the stairs again to discuss the plans when from across the street, came the voice. 'What are you lot up to?' shouted Wilma Craig.
'Aye, what are you lot scheming?' asked her pal Marion Taylor as they crossed over the road towards us.
'We're having an important meeting about where we're going and you two are no coming.' grunted Ronnie
'Going where?' Marion asked appearing to be uninterested.
'Err, we've not finalised the details yet,' was the reply.
'We've got a jam jar and a net for fishing,' said Wilma. 'We're going to Roseburn Park to catch minnows and redbreasts and my dad has tied a string around the rim of the jar so that we can carry the fish home,'
'For tea?' I asked sarcastically.
The girls looked at each other; unsure if I was being serious or not but scowled back, in case I wasn't.
'What have you all been scoffing?' asked Marion.
'Wagon wheels and there's nane left.' was the response from Billy. 'Yer fat enough anyway.'
'Dinae be cheeky you or I'll skelp yer jaw.' Wilma's message was clear and Jimmy along with the rest of us decided that no reply was the best option.
Not waiting for the girls to invite us to go fishing, I agreed on behalf of all the boys present that they, the girls could accompany us to Roseburn Park at Murrayfield, near the Ice rink and the more famous rugby ground. We set off by Haymarket, dodging tramcars as we crossed the road, passed the clock and the railway station.
When we arrived at the park, it was already crowded with mums and children enjoying the afternoon sunshine. Children were running about playing games and balls were bouncing everywhere. Some small boys were kicking a football but keeping it well away from the flower beds to ensure that the park warden didn't get upset. Adults were lying on the grass reading, sunbathing or just lazing in the warmth of the sun but the real attraction for older children was the nearby bubbling burn with small fish in abundance darting and swimming amongst the rocks.
With our shoes and socks off, the boys wearing jeans rolled them up above their knees whilst the girls tucked

their dresses into the bottom of their knickers. We all wanted to be the first to catch a fish and pop it into the jar held by Marion who stood with only her toes touching the water; insisting that she couldn't swim.
'Neither could I in water which was only knee deep,' I said but we couldn't persuade her to change her mind and step into the burn.
Although we could see minnows and the larger redbreasts swimming around our feet, we were hopeless at catching them in the net that the girls had brought along. A decision was taken to build a dam and sweep the shoals into a homemade pool. We cupped our hands below them as they swam by and tried to lift and throw them on to the bank but guddling was not at all successful. Eventually through perseverance rather than skill, we mastered the art of letting the net drift gently towards a shoal before sweeping it upwards to catch the unsuspecting fish. About eight fish of various sizes were now swimming round inside the jar, nibbling at plants which had been growing by the water's edge. We knew that they would be hungry.
As the afternoon stretched out, we lay on the bank enjoying the warm rays of the sun. We were talking about the oncoming bonfire season, having a laugh and a joke about our teachers and anyone else that came to mind; generally enjoying the happy atmosphere of the park when we saw the parky wandering around picking up litter with his long spiked stick and heading in our direction.
'What mischief, are you lot thinking of getting up to?' he shouted.
'None,' said Ronnie. 'Not us.'
'Good,' he said. 'Don't go throwing rubbish around now. I've enough to pick up.'
'Dinae bother then,' said Billy.
'What was that you said? Are you being cheeky son?'
'Oh! no,' I said scowling at Billy. 'He was just meaning that if people would put their rubbish in the bin over there, you wouldn't have to bother picking it up.'
'Aye yer right there,' he said as he passed us spiking the crusts from a piece on jam and placing them into his sack.
'I'm hungry,' said Billy.

'Me too,' was the unanimous response.
'Anyone got any money?' someone asked.
'No!' was the quick and despondent answer.
Jimmy had a brilliant idea. 'Why don't we go for apples on the way home?' he asked.
'Where?' asked Wilma
'In the gardens across the main road,' answered Jimmy, pointing in that direction.
'Do you mean pinch them?' asked Marion.
'Na! We'll just ask the owner if we can climb his trees and take home some of his apples to save him collecting them,' replied Jimmy with more than a hint of sarcasm in his voice.
'Do you think that he would agree to that?' and before she could say anymore
Billy interrupted her. 'Oh! he will. Now let's go.'
'Great idea,' Ronnie mumbled and as heads were nodded in agreement, we ignored the girls and took off across the park in the direction of the road and the apple trees.
'What about the fish?' asked Wilma.
'Just tip them out,' I shouted.
'What in the bushes?'
'In the burn,' I shouted.
'Oh right!!' she shouted back aggressively as she turned and ran towards the burn, accompanied by Marion.
We slowed down and waited for the girls to catch up. 'I'm keeping the jam jar,' said Wilma, there's a halfpenny return from the shop.
'Aye,' said Marion, 'there is.'
Murrayfield was a posh area and had high walls enclosing the gardens where the fruit and apple trees grew. Having climbed a few walls to review the situation, we found one garden that had numerous large red apples growing on a couple of trees close to the perimeter wall. The nearby plum tree was also full but as they were small and green they were not so tempting. To ensure success, a coordinated team effort was now required and It was quickly decided that as Jimmy and I were the two best climbers, we would climb the wall, drop inside and cross over the grass to the trees. Billy and Ronnie would sit on

the wall to pull us up on the way back. The girls would stay on the pavement and watch out for anyone coming down the road who might interfere with the operation.

I had tucked my jumper inside my jeans held up with my belt to keep the apples in whilst Jimmy's apples were going inside his zipped up jerkin. We nodded to each other and with a bit of help from the others, we were up and over the wall, crossed the grass and had shinned up the two beckoning trees before Billy and Ronnie were sitting on top of the wall. As we plucked the apples and stuffed them into their respective holding areas, we looked across at each other and grinned.

'Hurry up,' called Ronnie, in a low voice but which sounded to us as if he was using a megaphone.

The front of my jumper was now bulging and just as Jimmy and I waved to each other to indicate that we had picked enough, a window opened at the house across the lawn and a women's voice called, 'hoi! What's going on out there?'

'Somebody is shouting from the window,' warned Billy, sitting astride the wall.

'We hear them,' I replied. 'Get down and run for it Jimmy.'

We both dropped from the branches of our respective trees and wobbled as fast as we could over to the wall. Billy was now lying flat on the wall with his head and shoulders facing down into the garden. His hands reached down to meet Jimmy's hands stretching up the wall but there was an agonising gap.

'I hear a dog barking,' I roared at Jimmy and as I leaned my back against the wall, I shouted to him to put his foot into the palms of my hands which were clasped and resting on my right leg. 'Put your hands on my shoulders and push up,' I shouted which he did and as I turned inwards and lifted the sole of his foot upwards, he grabbed Billy's waiting hands and was pulled up on to the top of the wall.

'Right Ronnie, grab my hands. I'm coming up now.' I jumped upwards and felt Ronnie's hands clasp mine as I started to walk up the wall. It was then that I heard a man shouting out instructions to his dog and rude obscenities in my direction. As I edged up the wall, I felt the dog snapping and snarling at my heels. I didn't know if it was a Great Dane or a Jack Russell but I hoped that it was the latter. As I reached the top of the wall, Ronnie dropped down to join the others on the pavement but as I swung my legs over the top of the wall, I felt the tear and the rip down the right leg of my jeans;

'Watch out for that piece of barbed wire sticking out near the top of the wall,' shouted Ronnie.

'I've found it,' I assured him as I landed at his feet.

'Are you all okay?' asked Wilma with her motherly instincts coming to the fore.

'All in one piece,' I said, starting to share out the apples quickly for ease of running. The lads stuffed them down their jumpers whilst the girls placed them inside their blouses and as we took off down the street, I glanced over my right shoulder and saw a grey haired old man peering over the wall, shaking his fist and shouting something about kicking my erse for me.

With the apples moving and sliding around inside my jumper, I knew that I was losing some which were falling downwards and out through the large tear in my jeans.

Reaching home out of breath, we sat on the stairs and started to laugh. The apples weren't sweet but they were not bad and after all, we had helped the owners by gathering in the harvest for them albeit a wee bit early. We shared them out equally between the six of us and as we munched our spoils, we never once thought about washing them before we ate them.

'Hope that you have not been up to any mischief today,' said Harry Dingwell who lived with his brothers Johnny and Willie as he squeezed past us going up the stairs.

'No. Not us,' we shouted; 'just having fun.'

I hadn't yet decided how I was going to explain to my mother, the large tear in my jeans and wondered if her definition of having fun was the same as ours.

Chapter 35 - The Welcome

Comrie is a small Perthshire village about six miles from Crieff. My mother was born and raised there and my grandfather was a ploughman on a local farm. On school summer holidays the family would head for Comrie. Sometimes, we would stay in a bed and breakfast and sometimes we were very lucky to be given a bungalow loaned out to mum and dad from old friends.

Cultybraggen Army Camp in Comrie housed German prisoners of war who were often seen around the village carrying out general repairs and maintenance tasks under supervision of military guards.

One afternoon my mother decided to go for a walk up the country road towards the camp with myself holding on to the pram whilst my younger brother Ally sat gurgling in it playing with his rattle. As my mother approached a group of prisoners repairing a dry stane dyke, one of the prisoners asked the guard if he could say hello to me and was given the nod of approval. He told my mother that he had two children at home and was missing them very much and although his English was broken, my mother seemed to understand what he was saying.

'This is Howard,' said my mother pointing at me 'and this is Alistair his younger brother in the pram.'

'Guten tag Howard. Hello Alistair,' he said as he smiled and crouched down patting me on the shoulder. He took of his German army cap and placed it on my head, stood up and saluted me. I think I smiled. 'Please Howard can keep my hat?' he asked the guard. My mother told me later on in life that the guard had winked and turned away.

'Dankeschan for speaking to me and letting me meet your children, Frau. You have been very kind.'

'Thank-you for the cap and I do hope that you will be home with your family soon,' my mother replied. Prompted by

her, I think I said thank-you and waved goodbye as we went on up the road. 'Cheerio,' said mum looking back with a sad look on her face 'and thanks again for the cap.'
'Auf Wiedersehen,' he called
'Auf Wiedersehen,' shouted all his fellow prisoners.
As we passed the guard, my mother thanked him. He nodded and smiled.
The cap remained in the family for years and dad wore it when painting and wall papering the house.
Summer holidays in Comrie meant seeing old friends again like the twins Lachlan known as Lachie and Fiona Stuart. We had freedom to roam through the woods, climb trees, run barefoot over the fields and paddle in the burns which when dammed with boulders; we could swim in the pools. We played for hours in our secret hideaways, jumped off hay carts into stacks of hay in the fields and could always count on the farmhands to share their lunchtime piece with us.
One day as we lay in the afternoon sunshine watching a hare playing with her young leverets among the buttercups and enjoying the tranquillity of her field; oblivious to any danger, we watched as a little black speck in the clear blue sky circled nearer and nearer. Out of the sun the golden eagle dived, picked up a young hare and took off. 'Did you see that?' asked Lachie.
'Wow!' I said.
'That's nature as it happens,' said Fiona.
We lay for a while thinking of nothing but living for ever. Life in the tenements of Auld Reekie seemed another world away.
One day as our family travelled through Glenfarg by bus en route to Comrie, we stopped at the village inn to let people off the bus. Standing by the side of the road were some travelling people or tinkers as they were affectionately known. Tinkers travelled through Comrie and around Perthshire mending pots and pans, sharpening knives, scissors and garden shears and taking on any chores or odd jobs of work which were required to be done around the outside of the house; chopping wood and making clothes pegs were favourite tasks. They would often play a

tune on the bagpipes or tin whistle, sing folk songs or tell stories which had been handed down through their families for as long as anyone could remember. All they asked in return as they held out their palms or caps was fair payment for their completed tasks or something to eat and a few extra pennies.

They were close knit families and communities who lived with their horses and dogs by burns and streams where they could catch the odd trout and fetch fresh water at will. In the protection of the woods they built their lean-to shelters by bending boughs and saplings over and entwining them into an igloo shaped home which was then covered by branches and leaves. If available an old tarpaulin canvas or waterproof material would be thrown over the branches and weighed down with stones tied to ropes. Inside it was dark but warm and cosy. Mattresses to sleep on were made from sacking filled with grass, or straw.

One day Lachie and Fiona took me up to a camp in the woods at the back of their house to meet Patrick, Dougal and Flora MacPhee who were ages with ourselves and whom they had befriended three years previous. It was always about this time that they appeared and made their home in the wood. There were four families and nine or ten maybe even twelve children running around or carrying out chores. They all seemed happy, clean, well fed and were very pleased to see the twins who introduced me as Howard who had come all the way from Edinburgh to meet them.

'Good morning Mrs MacPhee,' called Fiona as Pheemy MacPhee came over to greet them.

'Hello to you both. My you've stretched Lachie and put on a bit of beef since I last saw you but you Fiona are as pretty as ever. I'm sure it's this Perthshire weather that just makes you blossom and this is Howard from Edinburgh, so I overheard. It's very nice to meet you Howard and you are all very welcome. Come away over, sit down by the fire Fiona and give me all the news,' she said, leading us over to a large smoked blackened cooking pot and an even blacker kettle which hung over the fire on a hooked pole and had belching steam rising from it. Now just call me Pheemy. Patrick you and Dougal finish feeding Nab and get him fitted into the cart ready for your dad. Make sure that the brasses and leathers are clean now.' Nab a piebald horse tethered to a nearby tree continued munching at his meal from a large wooden bucket oblivious to plans being made for him.

Although they had unkempt hair, patches on their jackets and jerseys, all the children looked glowing and healthy. They wore varieties of trousers, skirts, tops and socks; some worn inside out. Those who had footwear wore boots or brogues but all were carrying out their tasks around the campsite laughing and chatting continuously with childlike impish looks on their faces. At the edge of the camp by a large oak tree, an older boy Gregor could be seen strolling up and down practicing on his bagpipes which was often the best way to source a few pennies from the tourists.

'Here's a cup of tea,' said Pheemy as she handed each of us a tin mug with newly brewed tea swirling around the rim 'and a wee bit of shortbread left over from Hogmanay.'

'Thank you so much,' we all said together knowing that their supply of food was not in abundance.

Their dad Hamish who was tall and lean appeared wearing a dark brown cloth cap matching his jacket and trousers and with a shout of 'hello,' passed by and made his way over to where the boys were trying to back Nab into the shafts of the cart. His hair and moustache looked as if they had recently been trimmed but the long scar down his left cheek had a fearsome look and immediately drew one's eyes to his face. 'When will dad be back?' asked Flora.

'I don't know,' said Pheemy looking deeply into the fire. 'I'm not sure that he will be coming home for a while.'

Lachie and Fiona looked at each other with wide open eyes.

Hamish shouted cheerio to all the children pulling each of his boys close to him. He, ruffled my hair, gave a nod to Lachie and Fiona and held Flora in a tight hug before whispering something in Pheemy's ear; giving her a long lingering kiss before climbing up on to the cart. With a tug of the reins, Nab trotted on and with children running behind him Hamish gave a final wave without looking back. Pheemy pulled her shawl around her shoulders and holding her rosary in her right hand, she blessed herself with the sign of the cross. As she stood with her children cowering into her long grey skirt which hung down covering the laces of her well-worn shoes, I remember thinking how tired and pale she looked.

'Would you like to sit at the fire again?' Patrick asked his mother.

'No, I'm fine son, thank-you.'

She gave Hamish a final wave and a whisper of good-by as he disappeared down the track and it was only then that I heard the strains of the pipes playing 'Will Ye No Come Back Again' coming from beneath the branches of the spreading oak.

For the rest of the day we sat round the fire roasting tatties, eating bannocks and played some games in the woods until it was time to go home. 'Will you come and see us again?' asked Pheemy shaking my hand and giving all three of us a kiss on our cheeks. 'It's been lovely to meet you Howard and to hear all about Edinburgh. You will come again? I know you will and God bless you all and your families.' Tears were rolling down her cheeks as she wrapped Patrick, Dougal and Flora into her arms

The following summer, I went back with Lachie to the campsite but we never did see the family again. Lachie had heard about a death caused by someone from the camp; a man being arrested and sent to gaol but he wasn't sure of the facts. It could well have been Hamish. Adults didn't talk much to children about such happenings but there were many rumours around the village.

I have always remembered how little that family had but how happy they had seemed and how they had shared a moment in time with me, making me feel so welcome. I had heard of and had now experienced true Scottish hospitality shown to me, a stranger, albeit a young stranger who had entered the world of travelling people.

I didn't realise then that their way of life was passing all too quickly.

Chapter 36 - Life At Comrie

One day during the school holidays, my mother asked me if I would like to go through to Comrie on my own for a few days.
'On my own?' I asked, thinking that I hadn't heard right.
'Yes Howard, on your own, by bus.'
'Oh great,' I said; After all I was nearly nine and half years old.
'When?'
'How about Saturday morning?'
I couldn't speak which didn't happen very often. 'Will I need pyjamas?' I asked.
'Of course you will need pyjamas,' said my mother indignantly 'but don't worry, I'll pack your case and make sure that you have everything you need,' and when Friday night came my case was packed and ready. On Saturday morning we travelled by tramcar along Princes Street to the bus station at St. Andrews Square. Having said good-by to my mother and received a hug and a peck on the cheek I climbed the steps of the SMT (Scottish Motor Transport) bus where the conductor placed my small case up on the rack and I edged into a front seat by the window. I saw my mother having a chat with the conductor who looked at me, nodded and smiled. My mother waved to me as the bus pulled out to start my journey which would eventually lead to Comrie in the heart of Perthshire where my Auntie Mary would be waiting for me.
I changed at Falkirk where the conductor handed me over to the conductor of the Stirling bus who, when reaching Stirling left me in the care of the conductor of the bus bound for Crieff. It was an exciting journey as the countryside rolled by and I saw people carrying out their daily chores and life as it was in the many villages that we passed through. Although I had a corn beef sandwich and

some cake, passengers kept talking to me and giving me sweets and biscuits. As I got off the bus at The Square in Crieff and waited for the connecting bus to Comrie, I passed the time watching some old men having a laugh and enjoying themselves playing a game with huge draughts which were lifted and moved by hooking a long stick into a ring on each draught. The bus rolled in and the conductor jumped down to let the waiting passengers on. 'Where have you come from?' he asked as I handed him my ticket.

'Edinburgh.' I said

'All on your own. My, what a clever lad.'

I think I blushed. 'My Auntie Mary is meeting me in Comrie.'

'That'll be Mary Grant from Commercial Lane.'

'Do you know my Auntie Mary then?' I asked.

'Young man,' he said, 'in Comrie Everyone knows everyone. You'll be Doll's oldest lad Howard from Edinburgh. It's Doll's lad from Edinburgh,' he shouted to the driver.

'My he's grown came the reply.'

For the second time that week I was dumbstruck.

As the bus reached the village and passed up Comrie Main Street, the conductor pointed through the window; 'there's your Auntie Mary waiting for you at the top of the lane. Enjoy your holiday; I hope it's not too quiet here in Comrie for you.'

'Thank-you,' I shouted over my shoulder as I jumped off the bus and ran down the street with my small case in my hand.

'Come away in,' said Auntie Mary as we walked down the lane and reached the cottage. 'There's a pot of soup on the fire; I suppose you'll be hungry.'

I remembered my mother's words; Your Auntie Mary will be very pleased to see you but don't expect too many words nor hugs and kisses.

'Oh good,' I thought to myself and mum was right.

The cottage was very small with one low window at the front and two green doors which met in the middle when closed. My mother had told me that they were never locked

and only pulled too when Skippy the black and white collie was not allowed out into the lane; usually about the time vans from the bakery were pulling out of the lane on early mornings.
Off to the right was the main room containing a large double bed which Auntie Mary shared with Buntie her grown up daughter who worked in Crieff. In one dark corner, an old grandfather clock stood ticking away the hours whilst a table, four chairs and a sideboard could just be seen against the far wall, once my eyes were adjusted to the dimness of the room where the only light came from the glow of the log fire. Two old, high backed, arm chairs were placed either side of the hearth with a poker, tongs, and an array of pots and pans; a kettle, and a griddle sitting on or around the black grate. The smell of peat and the crackling of burning logs, created a warm, welcome into the house.
A steep set of stairs led up through the middle of the house to the attic which housed the bathroom and a bedroom whilst downstairs, the scullery housed the sink and cold water tap. All hot water came from the large black kettle which was continuously being boiled on the fire. Apart from the conglomeration of items that were stored in the bath and had to be removed when someone decided to have a bath, all other household items were kept in the scullery including bikes, logs, peat and an assortment of rabbits, pheasants and partridges which hung from the wooden beams of the ceiling.
Opposite the bathroom at the top of the stairs was the bedroom in which two single beds lay at one side of the room where Narth, Auntie Mary's brother slept in one; I was allocated the other. Under the eaves in the far corner of the room was a further bed where Aleck known as Son slept. In spite of having only one arm Narth rode his bike daily to and from his work at Cultybraggen Army Camp with varieties of game hanging over the handlebars; his pipe was usually dangling from his mouth.
My mother knew that it would be cold at night and had made sure that I had warm socks and a warm jersey to wear over my pyjamas. I think that I slept well, in spite of

Narth's snoring and talking in his sleep and forgetting to switch the light off when he returned from the toilet at least twice in the middle of the night. Skippy slept by the fire downstairs and roamed at will. Life circulated around Auntie Mary who's other brother Jim Grant, was my grandfather on my mother's side.
'You'll be off to see the Stuarts, I suppose,' said Auntie Mary at breakfast the next morning.
'Aye, I will,' I replied
'Well, keep out of mischief and behave yourself.'
'I will,' I shouted as I waved and ran up the lane towards the smiddy and headed for the Stuart's house which nestled into the hillside up the Lechcan near the farm where my grandfather worked as a ploughman.
'Hello young Howard,' said Mrs Stuart as she opened the door to my knock. 'I haven't seen you for ages. My! how you've grown. I heard that you had travelled through from Edinburgh on your own.'
I was speechless again.
'You'll be looking for Lachlan and Fiona? Well they've gone down to the field behind the railway line to help with the haymaking although I'm not sure help is the right word. You'll remember the field next to the one that you were tattie howking in last year.'
'I do Mrs Stuart, I'll find them. See you later,' I shouted as I ran back through the gate and down the hill.
The twins were about the same age and height as myself and always seemed to be bouncing with healthy energy. They were ruddy faced, full of freckles and always seemed to be laughing. With her long flowing red hair and kilt blowing in the morning breeze, I spotted Fiona first on top of the cart, pointing and shouting orders to a crowd of boys on the ground who were totally ignoring her. Then I saw Lachie with his sleeves rolled up, short trousers and a mop of tousled red hair sticking out from a tweed cap; he was jumping off a cart into haystacks with some other lads whom I recognised as coming from the village. They all seemed pleased to see me and within minutes I had impressed them with my bus journey through from Edinburgh on my own and I was joining with them in the

fun.
Half buried in a haystack, I heard my grandfather's voice, 'well Howard, you made it through on your own, I hear. Is your mother and father both well?'
'Yes thanks,' I replied and that was the formalities over.
'You can help me muck out Meg and Maggie's stalls to-morrow, if you have nothing else to do,'
'Can Lachie come too?'
'Can he use a broom and a shovel?'
'Oh aye,' shouted Lachie.
'If you want you can both ride on the cart with me tomorrow morning down to the village, after you've finished mucking out the stalls. I've got to get a few messages in.'
'We'll be up at the farm early,' I assured him.
'Right,' he said, 'I'll see you both tomorrow.'
My grandfather, like all the Grants from my mother's family was stocky and stood not much more than five foot six inches tall. His hair, what little he had was short and gray and sat comfortably on top of his weather beaten brow. When he spoke his teeth seemed to protrude a little from his mouth and his speech was always rather hurried. With his sleeves rolled up his small but strong hands and arms portrayed a long hard working life on the land. Between the pockets of his waistcoat dangled a silver watch chain with an engraved fob. A broad belt and braces held up his nicky tams, tied below the knees with rough string which tended to emphasise his bandy legs as he walked. Brown, buckled, leather gaiters stretched from below his knees, down his shins to his sturdy farm boots; forming a protection against the bumps and scrapes to his forelegs from farm life. A dark cap sat jauntily on his head to protect it from the sun and keep it dry on rainy days but as it looked so much a part of him I wouldn't have been surprised to hear that he wore it in bed. He had a deep knowledge of all things farming, especially ploughing of fields, horses, carts, haymaking, the seasons of the land, seeds sewn, crops grown and fruits harvested.
Meg and Maggie were huge Clydesdale horses bred for ploughing the fields and pulling the farm carts full of tatties, turnips and hay not to mention dung around the fields at

muckspreading times. The following morning while Grandad fed and watered them in the farmyard, Lachie and I mucked out the stalls with pitchforks and sloshed them down with buckets of water from the trough. Grandad had decided to leave Meg grazing as he fitted Maggie's harness on and backed her into the long shafts of the cart.

When all was ready we climbed up, sat on the long front seat and when Grandad grasped the reins and clicked his tongue for Maggie to walk on the huge spoked wheels turned and we were on our way downhill to the village. As we looked down on the hedges and meadows below us, it was like being driven around our estate, surveying all within. Everyone waved as we passed and shouted, 'morning Jim.' We waved back and laughed all the way down into the main street of Comrie where Grandad shouted, 'whoa! Maggie.' Outside the baker's shop, he passed me the reins and climbed down from the cart. Lachie and I looked at each other in awe and without saying a word, I passed one rein to Lachie whilst keeping a hold of the other myself.

Maggie obviously weighed up the situation and decided to show us who was really in control and trotted on down the street. Lachie and I pulled on the reins and shouted in our loudest voices, 'Whoa! Whoa! Maggie,' who continued to ignore us and trotted on. We were now in a state of panic as pulled on the reins and again shouted at the top of our voices, 'Whoa! Maggie, Whoa!' but to no avail and the huge wheels of the cart rumbled down the main street of Comrie.

Ronnie Macgregor the butcher, who was outside his shop talking to Mrs Robertson realised the situation, grabbed an apple from Tam Gillis's fruit and vegetable display next door and ran after the cart. Almost out of breath, he caught hold of Maggie's halter and shouted in a commanding voice from the bottom of his lungs, 'Hold up Maggie, woe!! That a girl,' He was obviously a natural with horses. Maggie saw the bright rosy apple and her horseshoes had sparks flying everywhere as she skidded to a halt on the cobbled street sending Lachie and me still holding the reins backwards over the seat and into the cart full of cabbages

and turnips which Grandad was delivering to the station master's house at the end of the village.
'Good girl Maggie,' said Ronnie, pushing the apple into Maggie's drooling mouth wishing that he had picked up two.
Grandad, hearing the commotion came running out of Macpherson's the bakers, red faced and spluttering with all sorts of words coming out of his mouth as he chased after the cart down the street.
'Take your time. Not so fast Jim,' shouted a couple of old cronies out on their morning stroll. When Grandad reached the cart he was almost bent double gasping for air and only his hands clutching the wheel of the cart, saved him from falling over. Finding an inner strength through embarrassment and anger, he reached up to Maggie's right ear and whispered in to it words of wisdom which I don't think were connected to the Ploughman's Initiation Ceremony of whispering and talking to horses but whatever they were both Maggie's ears pricked up and I'm sure she nodded understandingly.
'Are you alright boys?' asked Ronnie Macgregor standing up on the cart and looking down at us amongst the vegetables
'Aye we're okay thanks.'
'I'll let my two lads Ronnie and Murray know that you're back in the village Howard.'
The turnips and cabbages got delivered and when I arrived back at Commercial Lane late that afternoon, Auntie Mary commented about the commotion that had taken place up the street involving my grandfather's cart and two young lads holding the reins of Maggie.
'I heard about it,' I said and gave her a big smile.

Chapter 37 - The Accident

Between them the Stuarts and the Macgregors knew all the secret places in and around Comrie. They knew which birds nested in which hedges, where badgers and foxes roamed, in which streams the deer would drink from and where the River Earn could be dammed allowing us to swim in the pools. They knew the back road that led up to the Monument overlooking Lord Melville's Dunyra Estate where my mother had worked as a housemaid in her younger days. They knew the tracks and shortcuts through the woods which led to the Devil's Cauldron Waterfall and the Shaky Bridge which lived up to its name by swinging from side to side when walked across.

One afternoon myself, Lachie and a few of the lads decided to guddle some trout in the stream near the Shaky Bridge. Our skills at tickling the fish under their bellies and then throwing them on to the bank were not as brilliant as we had thought and after an unsuccessful ten minutes we made our way back to the rope swing near the bridge. We swung across the stream back and forth, singles, pairs and even three at a time laughing and laughing until with sheer exhaustion, we lay on the bank in the warm sunshine looking up at what we were sure was a golden eagle circling on the high thermals above the Monument. It was then that I spotted the large tree with its topmost branches hanging over the gurgling burn; almost touching the branches of a tree on the other side. I decided there and then to climb it and jump from one tree to the other. I had seen Tarzan in the films do it or was it Cheetah his famous chimpanzee; one or the other.

'Don't be daft,' said Murray Macgregor when I told him of my idea.

'You can do it,' shouted Angus.

I started my climb and reached the shoogly branches

leaning out over the stream; my knees shaking like the bridge itself. I steadied myself and wondered if I was daft but how could I climb down now especially in front of Fiona and Catriona who had walked up to the bridge to see what we were up to.
'Don't be silly,' said Fiona.
'Stop showing off,' said her best friend.
I was hesitating but the encouraging shouts from the lads below enriched my macho bravado. My mind was trying to work out the distance and how far I would have to leap before reaching the branches on the other tree.
'Ach!' I thought, 'I've got to go for it' and I did. With a Yodelling Tarzan like call, I leapt off the wobbly branch into mid-air and reached with desperate, clutching fingers for a beckoning branch on the other side. 'What a jump,' I thought and then it happened; the branch gave way and I crashed to the ground. There was a deathly hush as I lay on the opposite bank with my feet dangling in the water.
'Well done,' I heard Angus shout. 'You made it to the other side.'
I could hear feet running across the bridge. 'Are you alright Howard?' I heard Catriona ask with real concern.
'Aye,' I whispered, 'but I can't get up for that branch at the back of my leg.'
'It's sticking out of your leg,' said Murray. 'Just below your shorts, behind your knee.'
I was aware of the gang all crowding around me and peering down at my leg. The intake of breath from both the girls was frightening and set my heart racing.
'Can I help?' said a kindly voice which belonged to a man whom I could just see out of the corner of my eye. He was wearing a deerstalker hat, plus fours, walking boots and was leaning on a cromach. Seeing the bag slung over his shoulder, I guessed that he was a gamekeeper by trade. He knelt down, held the back of my knee firmly and with a comforting word, gently pulled from my leg what looked like a Douglas Fir to me.
'It's bleeding a bit,' said Euan as he peered over the heads of the others.
'Do you think he'll die?' asked Robbie

Everyone turned and glowered at him.
'I think that he's is going to be fine,' the man said in a quiet and confident manner as he pulled out a 'large coloured handkerchief from his pocket and tied it around my leg. Are you all from the village?' he asked, helping me to my feet.
'He's from Edinburgh,' said Lachie, pointing a finger at me, 'but he is one of our pals.'
'Ah!' said the man, 'you'll be young Howard then, Dolly Gee's lad. I heard that you were in Comrie again. Right let's get you up to the roadway, I've a large land rover and I'll take you down to your Auntie Mary's at Commercial lane. You can all squeeze in.' Auntie Mary had a look at my leg and cleaned it up with dettol. I tried not to whimper in front of the gang but I did with a pathetic look on my face. We all thanked Mr MacNab for his help and I promised to tell my mother that he was asking for her.
Next morning I limped up to the post office to buy stamps for Auntie Mary and by the time I walked back to the cottage, my limp had nearly gone although I still have a scar to this day.
The holiday was over so quickly and it was time to go home. I thanked Auntie Mary for looking after me and with a wave I headed up to The Square to catch the bus to Crieff and onwards to Edinburgh.
'See you at Hogmanay,' she shouted, 'your mother told me in her letter that you would all be through for the flambos. Give her my regards.'
'Oh great,' I thought to myself, 'back for the flambos.' All the gang were at The Square to see me off
'See you at Hogmanay Howard,' they shouted as they ran after the bus waving.
'See you then,' with a lump in my throat, I called back through the open window of the bus as it pulled away from The Square and rolled through Comrie.
I was homeward bound; feeling happy.

Chapter 38 - The Smiddy

My Auntie Kate's father was a well-known figure throughout Comrie and the surrounding rural area of Perthshire.

Jock Crearer was the blacksmith and he would allow me as a small boy to watch him shoe the horses and highland garrons brought in from the many farms and estates around Comrie. Many of the horses were huge Clydesdales used at the plough whilst the garrons carried the stags slung over their backs down from the hill.

I was always mesmerized when I entered the dark smiddy which was full of leaping fingers of flames erupting from the belly of the furnace casting shadows around the grey stone walls.

Smouldering coals were charged up by large bellows whilst clanging hammers on anvils echoed like distant church bells calling their flock to worship. Jock and his assistant moved among the huge Clydesdales muttering words into their ears as red hot shoes gripped by long iron tongs were carried from the furnace and placed on to the waiting anvils. The hammers crashed down on the shoes pounding the hot iron into the required shape and size sending sparks in all directions. The shoes were then plunged into large buckets of cold water causing rising steam and weird sizzling noises to fill this dark cavern with sounds, smells and dancing shadows creating the atmosphere of an enchanted world.

There was always lots of banter between the carters, ploughmen, farmhands, workers, gamekeepers, locals and Jock as the horses were led up the ramp from the street and in to the smiddy.

Sitting on a long solid dark wooden bench waiting to be used were a variety of metal tools necessary for Jock to apply his trade. There were huge pliers for pulling out the long nails from the old shoes, hammers of every size, levers, rasps and rough files, measuring devices, hooks, wire brushes and a myriad of other tools lying in nooks and crannies within the shadows and corners of the bench. Varieties of saddles, tack and horse brasses hung on the walls. Long handled brooms and shovels for sweeping and clearing up continuous piles of dung, lay side by side in a corner with metal bins whilst troughs of cold water for the horses that were always thirsty stood against the blackened walls.

Jock was tall and lean, with large gnarled hands and long arms which carried bulging muscles visible beneath his rolled up shirt sleeves. His aged tweed dark brown bunnet matched his waistcoat beneath his long leather stained apron. He had bushy dark eyebrows and the frown that he seemed to carry perpetually hinted at his lack of humour. It was known that he liked a dram or two of whisky and it was said that he never wore that frown when a dram was to hand.

He would stand facing the horse, step across the leg to be worked on, bend down and pick up the hoof to be shod, grip it between his knees, and prise out the nails of the old shoe. The hoof was then rasped down and generally smoothed into shape before the new shoe was fitted with precision ensuring that he retained his reputation as a craftsman.

There was always the real danger of Jock or his assistant being seriously injured as they moved around the horses; kicked or trod on, burnt from hot shoes or tongs, receiving the downward stroke of a hammer on the back of his hand or thumb not to mention sharp knives slicing or removing a finger. It was not work for the fainthearted but the hazards were accepted as part of the job.

Some horses stood still taking the whole operation in their stride but others were temperamental; resisting the poking and prodding at their hooves and spurred on by fear, they would kick out. These horses were led out to the green at the rear of the smiddy where ropes were lashed to tall wooden poles dug into the ground and spaced at intervals within a semi-circle. Two legs of the horse were tethered to

the ropes, leaving the third on the ground and the fourth for the blacksmith to work on.
To see these magnificent Clydesdale horses with only one free foot pawing on the cobbles, throwing back their heads and tossing their long mains whilst fear burned in their eyes and hot breath exhaled from their nostrils was sad. Their whinnying appeared to be a cry for help and they looked so sad; so very sad.
One day, under his guidance, Jock let me make an iron poker for the fire which sat in the hearth at home in Grove Street for many years. He also gave me a large horseshoe for luck.
As the use of the plough and the working horse faded away along with Jock, the smiddy was used for sharpening shears and tools and the making of ornamental fences, gates and such like. Gradually it became the small museum that it is to-day.
I still often think back to the days of the smiddy and the majestic horses that entered therein but I never did like that green.
Jock worked on until his finger, arm and knee joints bore the scars of arthritis and finally he succumbed to retirement. Daily he would pop into the smiddy as he passed by en route to collect his morning paper enjoying the banter with the lads whilst checking that their work was up to scratch. Gradually the visits became fewer as Jock's joints stiffened and he became housebound until he passed away.
Local people often swore Jock's spirit could be seen in the smiddy during the twilight hours talking to phantom horses whilst checking that their newly fitted shoes were a perfect fit.
The flambos were carried around Comrie to celebrate the oncoming New Year when families returned home and visitors came from all over the world to join in the fun. On such occasions, we went as a family by train and like everyone else when the train stopped at Kinross, we got out of the carriage and made a dash for the toilets on the platform; there were no toilets in third class carriages. Dad would buy tea and soft drinks to accompany the filled rolls

mum had brought from home. When the guard's warning whistle blew and the driver started up the engine, everyone stopped whatever they were doing and dashed back to the train. Mothers could be seen frantically counting their children before a member of the station staff went along the platform slamming the doors shut. The guard waved his green flag, blew his whistle again and the great wheels of the train were once again rolling into the heart of Perthshire.

In the early evening of Hogmany there were children's activities culminating in a fancy dress parade. Although after the parade the main street was deserted, the bars and lounges in the hotels were doing a roaring trade. About 11.30pm proceedings started to get underway at The Square; music was now being played from a caravan and revellers were keeping warm by singing and dancing. The pipe band arrived and started to tune up. Numerous decorated carts, tractors, varieties of floats bearing names such as The Young Farmers, Pony Club, and Rural Associations duly appeared and formed up in their allotted places for the parade.

Suddenly the flambos arrived and all eyes looked to them. The long narrow trees that had been cut down and stripped of their branches were propped up by the selected volunteers who waited patiently for the sacking which was soaked in liquid fuel and wrapped around the tops of the trees to be lit.

At midnight the bells rang out and everyone wished everyone else "A Guid New Year"

Men shook hands with men and women and children were kissed.

A rapturous cheer went up as the huge flambos were lit, bursting into flames and lighting up the night sky as they were hoisted by helpers into two waiting hands and rested against sturdy shoulders of local men. As the pipers led the parade down the street, they were followed by the floats, folk in fancy dress, and the flambos. A huge crowd of revellers arm in arm, singing, dancing, waving, kissing, cuddling and sharing a wide variety of alcoholic drinks with happy well-wishers lined the streets. Keeping the tradition

alive, families turned out to walk at the back of the parade and even women pushing prams joined in.
One year when the snow started falling, covering the roofs and lying thick on the streets, the whole scene took on a fairytale appearance of a village, in a land of mystique and magic.
The parade returned at intervals to The Square where the flambo carriers changed over before setting off again. It was completely baffling how Narth, auntie Mary's brother claimed his right each year to carry a flambo in spite of having only one arm and more than a few drams within his system but he did. I suspect he was closely monitored and assisted by members of the organising committee. The parade finally returned to the bridge in the centre of the village where the flambos were thrown into the River Earn for luck.
The merriment continued well into the wee small hours of the morning but by this time, we would be half asleep and on our way to bed.
Comrie was a special place.

Chapter 39 - Be Prepared

It was now time because of my age, to make a major decision in my life; should I graduate from the wolf cubs to the boy scouts? Should I give up my green cub cap, my jersey with all my badges and stars, my two fingered salute with my wolf cub howls of 'dib, dib, dib (Do It Better) and we'll do, dob, dob (Do our Best) and stepping forward with the left foot and right arm outstretched shout 'Woof!!' Exchange all that for an outdoor life of camping, singing campfire songs, moving up to a more senior world with my pals and shaking hands with my left hand. It was a definite yes!!

I accompanied my mother to the Scout Shop in Forest Road, near the University to purchase the yellow and brown neckerchief of the 152nd Gorgie Scout Group, shirt, woggle and scout belt to hold up my shorts. Under the Scout Master, Mr Mitchell who happened to be the janitor of our school, we met every Friday night in the school hall with his deputy, Senior Scout Leader Willie Moss and two scout leaders. Having enrolled and taken my promise, I took up my position at the end of the line and became a member of the Woodpecker Patrol. Meetings were on a Friday evening and started in a semicircle around the flag which was attached to the hot water pipe in the corner of the hall. With the unfurling of the flag, recital of the scout promise, a short prayer and the scout salute being given, the evening activities began. At the end of the evening we always sang the well known and popular hymn, 'Abide with Me,' being kept in tune by Mr Mitchell.

The scouts were to become a major influence in my life, for fun, fellowship, teamwork, adventures, discipline, camping, activities, sports, competitions, trying to win, knowing how to lose gracefully, daily inspections of kit at camp, washing dixies, lighting fires, tying knots, cooking, applying first aid,

singing around the camp fire and carrying out the patrol leader's instructions to the best of one's ability.
Dismantling tents when wet was a horrible task but an important part of our training. We were fortunate that we were able to hang them up for drying on the beams of the large store room at the school. Packing and pushing the trek cart, singing all the way to camp and most of the way home; all this and with my pals, laughing and laughing again; having fun. One of our favourite songs was:
'Over hill, over dale as we hit the dusty trail, the trek cart goes rolling along
Aye o ee that's the life for me, start the day and end it with a song
Where err you go, you will always know, that the trek cart goes rolling along.'
We learned how to stack the trek cart with all the camping gear required for a weekend at Bonaly Camp near Colinton, on the outskirts of Edinburgh. Walking, pulling and pushing, the huge wheels rolled and the cart trundled on; all the way until we reached our destination albeit exhausted. We daren't worry about the return journey. We took part in numerous competitions and left determined to do better the following year.
We progressed to long weekends on school holidays where we travelled by the SMT. bus to Lawhead Farm near Bigger. On dismounting at the farm, our equipment was unloaded and we made our way up the track, past the farm where the farmer's wife would come out to welcome us with a pail of fresh milk and a large tray of freshly baked scones.
We carried on our shoulders, our ex-army kitbags, the tents, guy ropes, poles, cooking utensils, dixies, shovels for digging out the latrines, bags of tent pegs and various other camping requirements up the track to the campsite. Our own personal equipment including sleeping bags, warm pyjamas, a small torch and loads of sweets and goodies had all been packed in a set order into our kitbags ensuring that on arrival at camp we could change quickly out of our uniforms, unpack our pullovers, shorts, plimsolls and waterproof capes if required and start to pitch the tents

quickly; especially if it was raining.
The selected site lay in a small valley near to a gurgling stream which provided running water and a nearby wood to allow us to collect deadwood for the fire. Setting up camp was hard work and required lots of teamwork but that first night at supper as we sat round our campfire with a mug of cocoa made from the fresh milk out of the pail, fried sausages, beans, buttered bread and strawberry jam scones, we felt good. We were happy and after the jokes, the laughter, the ups and downs for piddles outside at the rear of the tent in the cold dark nights, falling over each other as we tried to get back into the right sleeping bag; and more laughter, we finally zonked out to sleep. Reveille sounded at 0700hours by one of the leaders entering the tents banging on a large pot with a metal soup ladle. Having risen and turfed his patrol out of their sleeping bags the immediate task of the patrol leader assisted by his seconder was to get them down to the burn, ensure that they stripped off to the waist, washed, cleaned their teeth, combed their hair and were at the long dining table for breakfast on time at 0745 hours. I had been made a seconder and of course now, I had to lead by example and my teeth were grinding tightly as I slushed the cold water onto my face and under my arms.
After breakfast the flag was unfurled and the daily programme of activities was announced, commencing with the inspection of patrols who lined up outside their tents under their patrol leader. Points were awarded for clean tidy, uniforms, smart bearing, general alertness and for saluting the flag and the inspecting scoutmasters properly. The inside and outside areas were next and all tent flaps were rolled up and tied back; any litter left lying around meant penalty points being awarded. Sleeping bags which had been hung over a line outside to air were now rolled up at each person's bed space with pyjamas folded on top. Personal items of equipment such as cutlery, tin plates and mugs were laid out in front of the sleeping bags and were inspected for cleanliness. Rubbers or sand shoes were the norm for wearing in dry weather. If not being worn, shoes were brushed and sat in a row at the bottom of the tent

with the wellies. Groundsheets were shaken, brushed and left airing at the rear of the tents. I was very pleased when Alex Turner, my best pal from school decided to join the scouts and it was nothing to do with him having a good looking sister.

One day after lunch we were told to rest in our tents until a visitor had been to see us. We quickly discovered that Scout Leader John Hewit was going around each tent with a blanket full of small objects such as a coin, thimble, teaspoon, pen knife and much more; laying the blanket down inside the tent for about 10 seconds before gathering it up and leaving the tent. Each patrol had then to list the items that they had spotted. Points were awarded accordingly for observance.

As John entered our tent he tripped on the main guy rope and tumbled in head first. His bundle fell open and the enclosed items scattered everywhere. It took us sometime to retrieve and replace everything back into the blanket but needless to say, we won the competition. John organised plays, told stories at campfires and organised inter patrol competitions. He was a popular character and did a power of work behind the scenes; he was a true credit to the scouting movement. A scoreboard showed the running totals for all competitions leading to the Champion Patrol being awarded the trophy at the end of camp. It was all taken very seriously by ourselves as we took a pride in our patrols and wanted to be the best. At the end of the night, patrols would take turns at presenting plays around the campfire; afterwards we all joined in songs and laughter and the night seemed to roll on forever.

'Ging gang goolie goolie what's it.' was a favourite song by all but the words always seemed to get mixed up.

Cubs would have a day visit to the camp with the Akaelas to see, understand and enjoy what camping, fellowship and scouting was all about.

One evening at tea time we were informed that there was to be a midnight hike and that we would have to go to bed at 7 o'clock in the evening until 9-30pm when we would be awakened, required to get dressed quickly and be ready to move out of camp when called. Patrol leaders were to inspect their patrols and ensure that everyone wore lots of warm clothing, carried their small packs with waterproofs, hot drinks, biscuits, extra dry socks, a torch and a stout staff for support when walking. It had been decided that the route would take us to the top of the hill behind the camp. Mr Mitchell would carry the map and lead the way. The first aid kit would be carried by Skip Willie Moss who would bring up the rear with Scout Leader John. The two other leaders, Dave and Stan would stay behind to look after the camp and have a mug of hot cocoa ready for us when we returned. We set off marching uphill into the darkness singing, telling jokes, laughing and looking up at the sky and the stars. We bumped into each other trying to catch up and not get lost, especially after stopping for piddles. Up and up we climbed through the heather and around the peat bogs, past ghostly shapes of moving sheep in the darkness. As the mist came down and got thicker, the patrols roped up to each other around the waist. When we reached the cairn at the top, Mr Mitchell called a halt and announced the time as 10 minutes past midnight. A loud cheer went up as Skip and John came in at the rear. We all sat down by the cairn and snuggled out of the wind to open our flasks and enjoy our hot drinks and biscuits.

A few minutes had passed when Wally Broon, cried out 'What's that?'

'What's what?'

'That noise,' answered Wally as all ears cocked up and heads turned to look round at each other.

'I heard it,' said Mac. 'It was a wailing sound like ghosts or banshees.'

'It'll be the Pentland Ghosts,' Scout Leader John said, 'it's just about their time for walking on their hill.'

'OOOOEeeeee!!' came the scream through the swirling mist. We froze. Held our breath; not a sound from any of us as we looked at each other not daring to move a muscle.

'Aaaaeeeooo!!' it came again. We were rooted to the spot but suddenly as one, we huddled closer together and began to shiver in the cold of the night.

'There it is,' I shouted, pointing into the eerie darkness. 'I saw it move.'

'There's another,' screamed Albert Moray as a white shape moved forward and darted in towards us.
'Get off, keep away,' screamed Titch Cameron as we all stepped back nearly knocking the cairn over.
The ghostly white spirits were floating around us; darting in and out of the group as we cowered tightly into the wobbling cairn.
'Will they eat us?' asked Titch.
'They're no go'nae eat me,' said Rory MacDougal as he bent down, pulled up a muddy divot and slung it in the direction of the apparitions. The battle lines were now drawn and divots were heaved into the darkness in all directions.
'Ouch!, oh that hurt, aah! Ohh!' came the sound out of the darkness as the white ghostly spirits could be seen fading away quickly into the mist followed by a hail of wet muddy missiles.
We replaced the half dozen stones that fell off the top of the cairn and headed back down the hill; relating to each other what we had or imagined we had seen up there on the top. Everyone had their own version of the story but we kept looking back over our shoulders and were very glad to see the twinkling tilly lamps of the camp as we came out of the mist.
We were taken by surprise when striding up from the rear came Scout Leaders Dave and Stan and as they passed through the group, part of a muddy white sheet could be seen hanging out of Stan's rucksack. Suddenly it was all too clear but the tale of how the Pentland Ghosts were chased and ran for their lives frightened by a few brave scouts was talked about around the camp fires for years to come; no doubt the tale was exaggerated each time it was told.
Each morning a hand carved trophy was presented to the scout who had done most during the last twenty four hours to help others enjoy the camp. The trophy had a long handle with a large replica of a scout badge on top sporting the Scout Motto: 'Be Prepared.' It was varnished, polished, nicknamed the Jolly Hockey Stick and All boys were keen to win it. The leaders met each day to decide who it would

be presented to at breakfast the following morning. I had now been promoted to Patrol Leader of the Curlew Patrol and I was sure that I was being considered for it as my patrol had been winning a number of competitions and we were a very happy team.

The following day was the first aid competition and we were told that a hiker who had been passing by the camp had fallen on some rocks, was quite badly injured and lying on top of the small hillock, behind the kitchen area shouting for help; obviously in pain

All patrols were to stay in their tents until called forward to the start line. The draw was made. We the Curlews were last to go and I had the team fired up to win. Two judges were stationed on the hill at the accident point. Marks would be awarded for the approach to the patient, assessment of the injury, first aid carried out, leadership by the patrol leader, teamwork and the time involved from crossing the start line to carrying the patient back down the hill and crossing the finish line. The Curlews were called forward and sprinted up the hill knowing that the Eagles had a high score and a very fast time. We had discussed our duties whilst waiting to start and based on my assessment of the patient the necessary action would be taken.

The patient was lying precariously near the edge of the slope and as I approached, I spoke to him quietly; told him who we were, assured him that he was safe, would be looked after and would receive the help that he required.

'Donald you kneel between the patient and the slope to ensure that he doesn't roll off the hill.'

'Where do you feel pain?' I asked softly, waving the patrol forward and around me.

'Well done,' I heard one of the judges say.

There was no answer. I felt for a pulse and he was still breathing. I told the patrol that he was unconscious, did have a cut on his forehead and as his right arm was obviously broken, we would bind it to his side forming a splint thus preventing any movement as he was lifted on to the stretcher.

'Well done,' I heard the voice of the judge again.

'As his left leg also looks broken but there are no signs of any bones protruding, we'll bind that to his right leg,' I said. Issuing instructions to the patrol, they began opening the first aid equipment and whilst the patient's head was supported, his forehead was cleaned with dettol and bandaged. The limbs were bound with bandages and the patient was ready for lifting on to the stretcher.
'You are doing very well but time is running out if you want to win,' said the voice of the second judge in the background.
'Right everyone, round the patient and gently lift on my word as previously practised. Mac you and Callum hold the stretcher steady. That's good. Prepare to lift; lift,' I said and the patient slipped over on to the stretcher. 'Now prepare to lift the stretcher; lift.'
'Time's passing,' said a voice from the rear.
'It's no lifting.' said Bobby.
'We'll try again.' I said. 'Right on my count; 1, 2, 3, lift.' The stretcher lifted at three corners but not the fourth.
'Didn't even budge.' screamed Wally Broon looking at Titch's corner.
'I'll help Titch.' said Callum.
I quickly changed the team around. 'Mac you help Albert and we'll try again.' I said.
'Time is ticking away; 20 seconds left,' commented the judge.
'Everyone be quiet and keep calm,' I said firmly. 'Ready! 1, 2, 3, lift.' This time it moved off the ground but Mac and Albert's corner was too high and the patient almost rolled off the stretcher.
'We'll never get him over the line on time now.' said Albert
'We will,' said Donald Campbell as he stepped around the stretcher, took hold of the side and in one movement tipped it up. We stood dumbfounded and mortified as we watched our patient roll over the edge of the hill and disappear. We stepped forward, looked down and were horrified to see the patient hurtling down the hill, gathering speed and heading for the judge's table.
'I don't believe it.' spluttered one of the judges.
'Come on, after him.' I shouted.

'Look out.' shouted Mr Mitchell from behind the judge's table as the rolling body crashed into it sending papers, pencils and scorecards up in the air.
Out of breath, we reached the table.
'Did we make it on time?' asked Donald. I looked at him, closed my eyes, took a deep breath and shook my head.
Scout Leader Stan was quickly untied and in spite of his bruises was very forgiving saying that he now knew what it was like to be an Easter Egg but Stan had a pain in his left shoulder and it was decided to take him for a check-up to Penicuik Hospital six miles away. An ambulance wasn't needed as Scout Leader Dave took him over on the back of his motor bike which was no doubt another frightening experience for Stan.
The two visiting judges from the village who had been invited to assist with the competition, arrived breathing heavily and reported that until the moment when Stan disappeared over the hill, we had been doing very well with a chance of winning.
Mr Mitchell was rather displeased at the whole incident and pointed out that Scout Leader Stan could have been very seriously injured. 'Trying to win was one thing,' he said, 'but such enthusiasm as he had witnessed that afternoon would not be tolerated.'
Donald lost two days privileges to purchase from the tuck shop although he didn't go short. I didn't win the Jolly Hockey Stick but when we got back to our tent, we couldn't stop laughing.
Later that evening, Stan opened the flap of the tent and poked his head through. 'I hear that you didn't win the competition,' he said holding back the flap with his right hand as his left arm was in a sling.
'Are you alright?' I asked.
'I'm fine, just a bruised shoulder which is to be rested for a few days or so.
'I'm very sorry,' said Donald sheepishly.
'Don't worry Donald, you gained full marks for initiative.' Stan said kindly. I had to wait until the next camp before winning and being awarded the Jolly Holly Stick.
The normal woggle for holding neckerchiefs in place was

made of dark brown leather but whilst camping, walking, and carrying out projects in the hills we would pick up pieces of bone or wood, hollow them out and have our own personalised woggles.

Short trousers or kilts were the standard dress required to be worn with full uniform especially on church parades, parent's evenings and when travelling to and from camp on public transport. When camping abroad, kilts were encouraged to be worn. A scout knife carried in a sheath on the hip was accepted for general use at camp, adventure weekends, rambling and on various expeditions where it was an aid to carrying out numerous woodcraft skills and tasks.

A strong bough from a branch of a tree with a notch cut on top to support the thumb was a must for hiking; souvenir badges of places that one had visited were often glued to it.

A stout staff in one's hand, kitbag on the shoulder heading for camp with the rest of the troop whilst singing a hearty song was the source of the saying, 'Happy as a Boy Scout,' I think.

I took to the scouts like a duck to water and now led eight other scouts in the Curlew Patrol.

Chapter 40 - Fun And Fun

Throughout the camping weekends, each patrol, the Eagles, Falcons, Woodpeckers and my own Curlews were allocated tasks under the guidance of the leaders. Our toilets were within an allocated area away from the camp and behind a spread of gorse bushes. A hole was dug, used and covered up with the earth afterwards. It was quite common to see a body with a spade over one shoulder, carrying a toilet roll in his other hand heading for the area of the latrines whilst whistling or singing a happy tune. The stipulated rule was that one had to return by the burn and ensure that hands and the shovel were washed.

We learned to ditch the poles to allow the valance of the tent to sink on to the ground and be firmly pegged down, keeping us snug, warm and watertight.

Firewood was collected and the art of lighting a fire by rubbing two sticks together was taught although it was unanimously agreed that a box of Swan Vestas matches was more realistic. Rising Early to cook breakfast was a real chore for the duty patrol but peeling the spuds and scrubbing dixies, pots and pans after meals was a discipline in deed. All underpants and socks were washed in the burn and hung up to dry daily. Thank goodness it was a large and fast flowing burn.

Some of the highlights of the long two week camps were the arrival of the mail and even more important were the food parcels and goodies sent by our worried parents who knew that we would be hungry, starving and missing them so much. The parcels were opened and shared out at night when we were in our sleeping bags and supposed to be sleeping.

We did look forward to the arranged visit of our parents and the arrival of the coach at the camp but it was always accompanied by waves, hugs and kisses. How

embarrassing.
We showed them around the camp site, provided lunch, played games and hoped that some extra spending money for our various outings and the tuck shop would come our way. It was hard putting up with the farewell kisses and tears in front of our pals when it was time for them to leave but gradually they were coaxed into climbing on to the waiting coach. 'Look after yourself son; be good, Auntie Annie sends her love, and try not to miss us too much.' Kisses were blown towards us as we stood embarrassed looking at the coach.
'What's the driver waiting on?' I asked myself. The coach windows were now open and heads were hanging out of every window.
'Make sure your bowels are moved regular my wee lamb,' one old granny called out to wee Geordie Whitbread who nearly died on the spot. Although he was wee, Geordie was a piper in the District Scout Band and played well in spite of the drones on his bagpipes being almost bigger than himself. At last the engine started and the coach moved through the gates and down the road heading back to Edinburgh with arms and hands still waving out of the windows.
'Last into the pool shares his goodie box,' shouted, Titch Cameron.
'It's no me.' cried Bobby Douglas as we all turned and ran towards the pool that we had made by damming the river adjacent to the camp and that was that. Parent's Day was over.
Like the other patrol leaders, I tried to ensure that the younger lads; perhaps their first time at camp and whose parents couldn't make it, didn't drift off on their own, feeling down and dejected; even more important that they shared in our food parcels.
At camp we enjoyed a variety of exercises such as following trails set by the leaders, identifying various birds from their sightings, their calls and photographs. We identified trees from their leaves and tracks from animals not to mention making casts from their spoors. Tying a variety of knots whilst learning the practical application and

being taught first aid were popular. We played volleyball, quoits, swam in the river, swung across and leapt off a Tarzan swing into the river; enjoyed cricket, rounders and of course football.

We had some very good players in our scout group and a decision was taken to enter the Scout District League. Our hopes were high in doing well; finishing high up the league and possibly winning the cup. When we heard that Skinny Reece, a new lad into the scouts told us that he was a trialist for Hearts as a goalkeeper, our hopes soared. Our first match was against the bottom team in the league from last year and when our team ran on to the pitch with Skinny in his bright yellow jersey, white shorts, brand new gloves and a tweed cap on his head our confidence rose even more. We lost the match 23-0 and went home on the bus glaring at Skinny.

'It was my cousin that had a trial for Hearts,' he insisted.

The following year we came second in the league and won a 5 aside competition.

Bob A Job Week arrived once a year when scouts went round houses offering to do any odd jobs or chores such as cleaning shoes, gardening, chopping firewood or running errands for a bob. A Job Card was signed by the householder and a shilling popped into the box. Usually the rounds were done in pairs and mostly because of our uniform we were made welcome at the doors, sometimes with sweets and cakes. People were very supportive knowing that the money was going to scout funds and well deserved charities.

One day we called at old Mrs Gray who asked us to run down to the shops for some messages, clean the brass nameplate on her door and her tarnished bell which was on the wall outside the front entrance to the stair. Having completed the jobs, we went to get our card filled in and signed but found her bent over and holding on to the banister outside her front door on the top landing. She was coughing, wheezing and trying to stem the tears running down her cheeks. She assured us that she was fine but we didn't have the heart to take the money from her and said that we would collect it next year.'

'Do you think she'll be here next year?' asked Ronnie.'
'Don't ask,' I said and ran back to tell my mother who went up the street to tell her daughter.
Preparation for our two week camp in the summer holidays started weeks before; checking that all tents were in good condition and watertight. Poles, pegs, dixies, pots and pans etc. were on the check list to be loaded on to the lorry on the morning of departure. Thank goodness, chosen sites had built-in toilets and we didn't need to worry about that equipment.
My first long camp was to Enochdhu which nestled into the hills between Pitlochry and Blairgowrie and when the lorry was packed with the heavy equipment and the tents stacked high around the sides, we squeezed down into the middle which had been divided into two sections. Big cheers from all on board went up as we left; waving to all the mums and dads who were now looking forward to a glorious, peaceful two weeks. My introduction to the long camp was nothing short of fantastic and I was sold on the life of scouting.
At Helensburgh we nearly got eaten alive by midges swarming off the Gairloch and at certain times during the day, we walked about with towels around our heads and faces but it didn't stop us enjoying ourselves. The following year we camped in the border hills of Selkirk and the year after that; it was, two weeks in Aberdeen.
We left the port of Leith on a fishing trawler at night, bound for the granite city of Aberdeen. The crew made us welcome and kindly shared their supper with those of us who could face fish and chips, followed by steamed syrup pudding. Needless to say, it wasn't long before there was a long line of boy scouts hanging over the ship's rail being sick. As the crew, heading back to Aberdeen were fishing throughout the night, their bunks were available for us to sleep on albeit doubling up top and toe. Aberdeen harbour was a welcome sight the following morning.
That fortnight, the weather was fantastic and we swam in the outdoor pool, played various sports against a scout group from Ayrshire and sang with them as we sat round a campfire in the evenings. We loved Aberdeen and found

the people to be very friendly and welcoming.
The day before we left, it rained and rained. Everything was soaking and a decision was taken to move into a large barn on the farm adjacent to the campsite and offered to us by the farmer. The tents were taken down and hung up over the rafters to dry out ready for packing to go home the following morning. We slept in our sleeping bags amongst the hay and laughed and talked most of the night. We were up at dawn the following morning and had an early hot breakfast cooked on a fire outside the barn. The rain had gone off and the skies looked promising for a dry day. We were all excited at going home and packed our presents carefully. The camping gear was packed and loaded into the luggage compartment with our kitbags. We boarded the bus and headed through Aberdeen to the harbour and the waiting trawler. We waved and people waved back.
Scout Leader John said that he would do a final check of the campsite and the barn area for litter; the farmer had offered to drive him down to the quayside to meet us there. We had wonderful memories of our camp but little did we know that the excitement was not over yet.
The trawler was loaded and all boys and leaders were accounted for, except Scout Leader John. We leaned over the rails looking up the pier but there was no sign of him and the skipper of the trawler kept looking anxiously at his watch. After a long discussion with Mr Mitchell and the leaders, it was decided that the trawler which was now late, would have to move out of its berth and make way for another boat which had been allocated that particular berth and was waiting in the middle of the harbour to come in. Our trawler was to move and reberth further down the pier. The engines were started, revved up and as the boat edged slowly away from the pier who should come running down the jetty but Scout Leader John. Dave was shouting that we were only moving a short distance down the pier to a new berth but John was worried and upset and didn't seem to hear him.
We all started shouting and pointing down the pier which only seemed to confuse him more and to our horror he stopped running; took a few steps back, seemed to take a

large breath and started running towards the moving trawler. He took off and with his legs cycling in the air, his kilt above his knees, his arms outstretched and his hands reaching for the boat, he resembled an Olympic long jumper going for gold. His fingers clutched at the side of the trawler as it bobbed up and down in the swell and his feet dangled over the side as if he was doing an out of control Highland Fling. With greased lightning Stan and Dave leaned over the side and hauled him aboard.
'Are you alright?' asked Mr Mitchell, as John lay panting for breath on the newly scrubbed deck.
'Aye, I'm fine but there must be an easier way to come on board.' was his response.
Shortly afterwards we sailed for Leith and home with another memorable tale for the campfire.
The following year it was decided to go abroad and a real buzz circulated around the scouts. Parents and scouting officials of the Gorgie District had all agreed to help with the fund raising and the organising of the trip. We were going to Holland. Jumble sales, beetle drives, washing windows, running errands and a whole host of activities were organised to raise money. Kilts were to be worn and families spent some considerable time borrowing kilts and altering them to fit.
A lot of planning was involved in moving a party of thirty six excited boy scouts and seven leaders by overnight train to London, onwards to Harwich and across the North Sea by boat to Amsterdam where we would be met by a party of Dutch scouts with a coach to take us to our first hostel. Rotterdam, The Haig and Utrecht were some of the places that we were to visit. As we were to sleep in scout halls and hostels, we didn't have to worry about carrying tents across the North Sea. It was a big adventure and we were all excited about the trip. On the Friday of our departure, we couldn't wait for school to finish and the long summer holidays to start. We were leaving on the 8pm train from the Waverly to Kings Cross and all our kit had been ready and packed for days.
I was now in my first year at Boroughmuir Senior Secondary School and was on a bit of a high about the

school holidays and leaving for Holland that evening. I was laughing and talking in the classroom when the teacher after shouting 'quiet,' decided to make an example of me to the rest of the class. 'Can you not help showing off or do you just enjoy it?' he yelled at me.
'No sir,' I said in a quiet voice with my head bowed. 'I'm sorry sir, I didn't hear you.'
'I know that you're not deaf. I hope that you'll remember this punishment and that you will have learnt to listen when you come back from the holidays. I don't take any pleasure in having to use my brand new very expensive belt and you should be ashamed that you are the first to experience it.'
He turned, opened his desk drawer and took out the long, thick, dark brown, leather belt which separated into two serpent like tongues at the end.
'I won't take any pleasure from this either,' I thought to myself
I had two double handers and tried not to winch as I made my way back to my desk.
When the bell rang, we all ran outside and threw our schoolbags up in the air.
'Was that sair?' asked Wally Broon.
'I felt it myself,' said Albert.
'No,' I lied as the class gathered round me patting me on the back.
'Oh! I've left my library book in the classroom,' I said. 'See you all at the hall for roll call tonight at 5 pm and it's Holland here we come.'
After making sure that everyone was present, properly dressed and all items of kit were packed as required, including our passports which had been checked and double checked by parents and handed over to Mr Mitchell, we were ready to move. We left the hall by patrols at intervals to catch the tramcar along to the Waverly Station where the carriages were booked. All parents and well wishers who wanted to wave us off were going direct to the station.
The rucksacks which were required for this camp, were packed into the guards van and we climbed aboard the London train. None of us had been on an overnight train

nor even been to London before. We piled into the carriages reserved for us, pushing up the arm rests in an attempt to squeeze our pals into the seats. We also wanted to sit as far as possible from the carriage which our leaders had chosen. As instructed we wore football shorts under our kilts which allowed us to take our kilts off, fold and lay them on the racks above our heads beside our small packs which were filled with sandwiches, drinks and goodies. To cheers, waves, shouts and blown kisses, the train crept slowly away from Platform 11 en route to Kings cross. Spirits were high as we settled down for the ten hours journey ahead.
'How's your hand Howard?' asked Wally relating the story for all to hear.
As I reached up and took down my small pack, I knew that all eyes were on me. I opened it up slowly and uncurled a long, dark, leather, snake like object.
'Wow!! Let's have a look at that,' was the immediate response from Albert. 'I've felt one on my hand but never held one before. It wasn't a library book that you went back for then?'
I looked at him and smiled.
'I didn't realise it was so thick,' said Callum Smith. 'Let's have a look at your hand Howard.'
I held it out appreciating the all round intake of breath and accepting the moans of sympathy; it was red and a bit swollen. I passed the belt around for everyone to hold, touch and feel; inspecting it like a valuable antique.
We all laughed when Mac commented that it was nearly as big as both Titch Cameron and Geordie Whitbread together.
'Well,' I said, 'It's not going to cause pain to anyone else, ever.'
'How do you mean?' asked Callum.
We were now heading for the Border with the white horses of the North Sea on our left and as I wound down the window, I hesitated briefly before launching the evil looking belt into the darkness of the night. A huge cheer went up which brought Skipper Willie Moss down the corridor. 'What's going on?' he asked sliding the door wide open

and peering inside.
There was a hush as we looked up at his suspicious face.
'Nothing,' we all replied as one.
'Just having a belting time.' Bobby remarked casually.
With his left eye shut, he looked slowly around the carriage before suggesting that we settle down for the night. 'Try to get some sleep and do remember that there are other passengers on the train. Oh! and shut that window,' he said as he left closing the carriage door behind him.
'Yes skip.' we shouted as we tried but failed to contain our laughter.
In Holland, we toured the sights and ate raw fish standing on various quay sides as was the custom. We played football against other scout groups, gave displays of Highland Dancing which we had practised before leaving and listened to Dutch songs whilst responding with renditions of the 'Bonnie Banks Of Loch Lomond' and 'We're No Awa Tae Bide Awa' as we sat round numerous campfires.
We bought presents to bring home and had a fantastic time. We made many friends and looked forward to the time that we could reciprocate the hospitality when they visited us in Scotland.
'Thank goodness for camping and fun,' I remember thinking to myself.

Chapter 41 - Carmine

I was now twelve years of age and attending Boroughmuir Senior Secondary School where I had met lots of new friends; some who came from Gilmerton, a village on the south side of Edinburgh and others from an estate called The Inch. We played rugby, football, cricket, took part in athletics and many other school activities representing our Houses of which I was in Hartington. We enjoyed representing the school in competitions against other schools and I was often invited to their homes for weekends. I was astonished at the freedom of living in the countryside where one could play football in various fields and parks as opposed to the streets and back greens of Grove Street.
One day I arrived home from school and my mother said that she had some exciting news for the family. Sitting me down on the settee with Ally and Eleanor, we assured her that we were ready to cope with whatever it was.
'We have a new house and we are moving to The Inch,' said my mother.
'Where?' asked Eleanor.
'Why?' asked Ally.
'Fantastic.' I said. 'When?'
'In a few months,' said my mother. 'We're going to have a house with a toilet, a bath, three bedrooms, a separate kitchen, a front door, back door, a walk in coal cellar and a front and back garden.'
There was silence. We looked at each other in amazement and said nothing.
'Howard you will still go to Boroughmuir and Ally and Eleanor will go to schools nearer to the new house. Are you all pleased with the news?'
'Yes!!' we all shouted. 'Oh yes.'
'Will I be able to stay in the scouts?' I asked my mother.

'Of course you can, but like school, it will mean a bus journey. Perhaps some of your new friends from school would like to join the scouts.' and they did.
Dad had a friend who owned a large van and there was great excitement when it rolled up on the Saturday morning of the move. The neighbours helped to carry the furniture from the top flat down and around the tight bends of the stair. The mattresses, armchairs and the settee were the most difficult to manoeuvre but we eventually managed to get them out to the waiting van which was laden to the hilt; not another item could be squeezed in. Ally travelled in the front of the van with dad and his friend who was driving. Mum, Eleanor and I left Grove Street after many farewells, much weeping, and promises made to keep in touch with the neighbours. We travelled by bus to The Inch where all the streets were named after titles from the books of Sir Walter Scott.
That night we had baths, slept on mattresses in various bedrooms and woke up to birds singing from the rooftops. Mum and dad quickly met the neighbours of the surrounding houses who like ourselves were all moving into their new homes from all over Edinburgh.
The following afternoon the lads from school turned up at the door with football boots hanging round their necks and one with a football under his arm. 'Are you coming out for a game Howard?'
'Where?' I asked instinctively.
'Down at the park. We'll meet the rest of the lads there.'
'Oh great,' I said. 'I'll just check with dad that he can manage without me. I maybe should have been disappointed that he said 'of course,' he could but I was off before he changed his mind. A new and exciting life had begun for myself and the family.
With two of my pals, for ten shillings a week, I started delivering milk from a dairy in Marchment which was about fifteen minutes in the bus to Salisbury, five minutes on a tramcar to the shop which wasn't far from the school; we had been issued with school travel passes. The bottles of milk and bags of rolls were made up and placed in the wooden carts, ready for delivery when we arrived at 7am.

Although it was an early start, we finished our rounds and arrived at school with lots of time to play football in the playground before the bell rang. I used to whistle all the way up to the top flats, run all the way down the stairs or slide down the banisters to the stairwell and run outside as quickly as possible, hoping that no one had pinched a bottle of milk from my cart in my absence. Before long we moved along the road and progressed to delivering papers with a rise in wages to fifteen shillings a week. On arrival at the shop, the papers had their stair numbers marked on them and were sitting on the counter in their bundles ready for delivery. The front doors of the tenements were opened by our latch keys and delivery meant climbing the staircases and turning into winding corridors and dark alcoves to push the papers through the letter boxes. A bit scary at times.

Dad had learned to drive and purchased a small maroon Ford Anglia car which was a great asset to him in reaching his office at Abbey Hill where he was now working for the Social Services. Mum had a telephone installed and next to it on the table sat a wee box for the neighbours to put their pennies into when they asked if they could use the phone. Dad bought for the family, our first television set which was a black and white Defiant from St. Cuthbert's Co-operative Store where mum qualified for her dividend twice a year; our store membership number was 30641

One morning, shortly after moving to The Inch, an attractive girl appeared from the house directly opposite ours and after a courtesy hello and a few passing waves, quick chats developed into lengthy conversations and first names were exchanged. I just loved her name Carmine; she had been named after her Italian Grandfather known to the neighbours as Charlie and although our schools were in different directions, our paths seemed to cross more and more. I did admire her so much that one day I plucked up the courage to ask her if she would like to go to the pictures with me.

'What's in?' she asked.

'She Wore a Yellow Ribbon, a cavalry and Indian starring John Wayne at the Rutland.' I said

‘How about South Pacific at the New Vic?’ she suggested.
‘Great.’ I said. Saturday night was agreed upon. I worked out the money that I needed for return bus fares, cinema tickets, chocolates and ice cream at the interval; after all I had to make a good impression. When we arrived, I didn’t even have enough money to get in. I had based my estimate by mistake on matinee prices for children and the woman at the kiosk wouldn’t accept that we were under the relevant age. I was very embarrassed but Carmine opened her purse and paid the required entry fee. On the way home on the bus, I did manage to persuade the conductor to only charge us for two halves. That was our first date and ‘Some Enchanted Evening’ from the film became her favourite song; we did enjoy the film and each other’s company very much.
The years seemed to roll by quickly and I was now fifteen years of age when I decided to leave school against my parent’s wishes; earn some money and try out the big new, exiting adult world. I started in the grocery department of St. Cuthbert’s and although I won the Best Apprentice Award at night school studying sales, accounts and stocktaking, I was restless and wanted something more adventurous.
Carmine too had left school and started Nursing College and I remember thinking how suitable her caring nature would be for nursing and how attractive she looked in her uniform.
Rock and roll had arrived from America with the film ‘Rock Around the Clock’ starring Bill Hayley and The Comets. It was about then that Carmine and I started spending more time together, playing and listening to the records of Tommy Steele, Cliff Richards, Elvis Presley, Fats Domino, Little Richard, Buddy Holly and many more singing stars who were bringing a new sound and beat into our homes; encouraging the young folks to sing, dance, go out and enjoy themselves. The Palais at Fountainbridge had special cheap Friday night prices and was very popular for jiving and rock and roll.
One of the dress fashions around at the time was Edwardian Suits or drape suits worn by groups nicknamed

Teddy Boys who wore long jackets down to their knees, bootlace ties, drainpipe trousers which clung to their legs with very tight bottoms. It was often said although not to their faces that they had to unscrew their feet to pull their trousers on. They wore thick, crepe soled,
suede shoes, known as brothel creepers with bright coloured pink, orange or green socks. They had a huge wave at the front of their hair and at the back a D. A. (duck's arse) named because it was swept back at the sides and met in the middle; just like a duck as seen when it's diving for food below the surface.
Some gangs kept open razors behind the lapels of their jackets to use in gang fights or maybe it was just to show off.
One such Edinburgh gang who frequented the Palais, called themselves the Valdor Gang and they were there in force, the night that the American sailors who had docked at the port of Leith came up to town to enjoy the night life of Edinburgh. They had come for a good time which included meeting girls who wore coloured tight fitting jumpers and flared skirts which didn't leave much to the imagination as they danced and twirled around the floor. Seamed stockings held up by suspenders, flat shoes for jiving and pony tails were the fashion of the day.
Carmine and I had decided to go dancing the night that the Yanks came to town. We had waited in the separate male and female queues to hand in our coats to the cloakroom attendants and then moved into the main ballroom to sense the feeling of the night. The floor was already packed, dancing to a live band, which changed every hour on the revolving stage and we moved upstairs to buy a couple of soft drinks at the bar and leaned over the balcony to watch the dancing and see if there was anyone we knew
'There are a lot of American sailors in.' I said.
'They seem to be enjoying the jiving.' said Carmine. 'They are great movers and very lively.'
'I notice that the girls are flocking around them not only at the bar but on the dance floor.' I pointed out showing off my powers of perception.
Suddenly a chair was thrown from the balcony down on to

two sailors who were dancing with one girl in the middle of the floor. Heated words were exchanged and a skirmish broke out. Looking over the balcony Carmine and I had a ringside seat, so to speak.
A coloured man who had huge shoulders and was a giant in height was the obvious leader of the visitors and with a sweep of his hand, he waved all the sailors around him into the middle of the floor where they took their navy belts off and started swinging them round their heads daring anyone to come and get them. The Teddy boys, in strength were now circling their prey and when some glasses were rained down from the balcony bar, the spark ignited the charge into the centre of the dance floor and a full blown punch up began.
The band stopped playing. Arms and legs were flailing everywhere on the floor, screaming girls jumped out of the way as bodies were lifted up and thrown out of the circle on to the edge of the floor whilst a large crowd including ourselves watched from above in awe. Suddenly through the doors came the Edinburgh City Police followed by a host of American Military Police who waded in with truncheons and batons swinging. Gradually one after another, the combatants were dragged, some with black eyes, some with bleeding noses but all dragged in one direction to the Black Marias waiting outside. The Teddy Boys were taken to the cells at the High street and the sailors to their ship at Leith where no doubt, they were thrown into the ship's brig.
The dance hall was cleared and tidied up. The band started playing and everyone was jiving again. What a night to remember.
One cold frosty night, Carmine and I returned, rather late from the cinema and as we both had early morning starts, we agreed not to bother with a coffee in my house but rather to have a quick chat about plans for the weekend. To get out of the cold biting wind, we stood in the long dark vennel between my house and our neighbours. Just as we had given each other a cuddle and had started our goodnight kiss, a large dark shape came bounding through the entrance and nearly knocked us off our feet. We were

just recovering when a body came running through and bumped into us shouting, 'come here Jupiter. Oh hi! Howard. Hello Carmine.'
It was Elspeth from next door who had taken her dog for a short, late night walk. 'Sorry,' she said as she breezed through, opening and slamming her back door behind her. What a fright we got, not to mention the spoiling of our goodnight kiss. We did laugh about it afterwards and from that night on, if we weren't going into one or the other's houses, we stood in Carmine's vennel where there were no dogs likely to spoil our fond goodnights.
Carmine and I were enjoying each other's company and found ourselves spending more and more time together. Sometimes on a Sunday morning, I would chum her to the chapel and to special services such as Midnight Mass on Christmas Eve. Sunday morning walks were followed by lunch at her house which was nearly always, the real Italian spaghetti with a roast and served Italian style. Often the whole family turned up and there was always enough for everyone. This custom was introduced by her Grandfather who had come over from Italy with her Grandmother many years before to settle in Scotland. He started his own business in ice cream, chips and general catering and if anyone could prepare authentic Italian meals, it was Carmine; known to everyone as Charlie. I remember him telling me one day, why he had nicknamed his granddaughter as 'three penny bit'. It was because, she was always asking for three pence to buy sweeties. I loved old Charlie who was a real character with a handlebar moustache and always wore a flat bonnet whenever he appeared out of doors.
Unfortunately, time was catching up with Charlie and he was requiring almost full time care. Carmine took the very difficult decision to give up her nursing studies to look after her grandfather but after he had passed away, she did apply to start work as a doctor's receptionist. Doctor and Mrs Thomson turned out to be true friends and a source of guidance to her for years to come; with their three children they were indeed a lovely family.
My family were all settling into our new life at The Inch and

getting on so well with the neighbours. Hogmanay meant a party every night in a different house with singing accompanied by someone on the piano or the accordion. Dancing, drinking and socialising continued well into January and everyone seemed happy but I was restless.
One afternoon as I passed an army recruiting show at the meadows, I walked around the marquees, spoke to the soldiers in combat dress, held various rifles and pieces of military equipment, watched films of the countries where the regiment had been stationed and where they could be posted to in the future. Serving around the world appealed to me and I was hooked especially with the red uniforms and the large bearskins of the Scots Guards.
At seventeen and a half years of age, I took the Oath of Allegiance to Her Majesty the Queen at the Army Recruiting Office in Queensferry Road and left on the ten o'clock overnight train from the Waverly Station to London. It was the 11thJune 1959, the day before Carmine's seventeenth birthday.
I said the goodbyes to my family and had tears in my eyes as I held Carmine close and said farewell to her at the station.
I arrived at Kings Cross in the early hours of the morning and took a taxi over to London Bridge Station where I caught the train to Caterham and a bus up the hill to the barracks.
As a huge wall and a number of iron gates came into sight, I asked the driver, if he would please let me off at the correct entrance to the Guard's Depot.
His response, in a broad cockney accent was that, 'The Guards Depot lad is next door to the local asylum and whichever gate you go through, once you are in, there's not a lot of difference.' He winked at me and wished me good luck as I stepped off the bus.
With a small suitcase in my hand, I passed through the main gate and entered a world of uniforms, marching, drill parades, kit inspections, saluting and discipline. I was now a raw recruit in the Scots Guards and my army career had just begun.

Printed in Great Britain
by Amazon